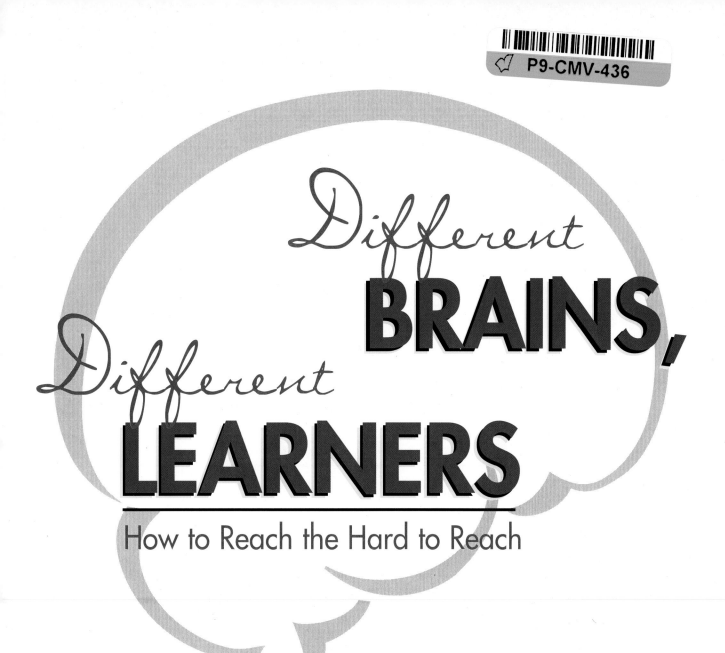

Different **BRAINS,**
Different **LEARNERS**

How to Reach the Hard to Reach

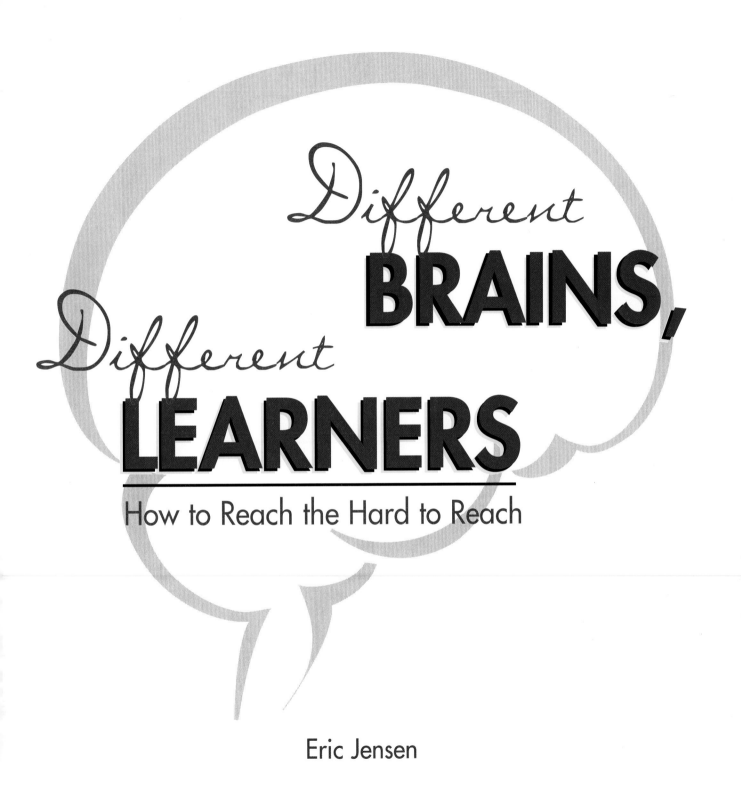

Different BRAINS, Different LEARNERS

How to Reach the Hard to Reach

Eric Jensen

©2000 The Brain Store
Different Brains, Different Learners

Tracy Linares: Layout and Design
Karen Markowitz: Managing Editor
Gail Olson: Assistant Editor

Brain SPECT Images courtesy of: *Images into Human Behavior: A Brain SPECT Atlas*, Daniel G. Amen, MD, 2000.

Printed in the United States of America
Published by The Brain Store, Inc.
San Diego, CA, USA

ISBN #1-890460-08-7

For additional copies or bulk discounts contact:

The Brain Store, Inc.
4202 Sorrento Valley Blvd., Ste. B
San Diego, CA 92121
Phone: (858) 546-7555 • Fax: (858) 546-7560
E-mail: edubrain@connectnet.com
Website: www.thebrainstore.com

NOTE: Human behavior is an ever-changing science. New technology, better drugs, more reliable clinical research and increasingly practical interventions are constantly emerging. This having been said, the author and publisher have checked with multiple reliable sources to ensure accuracy and industry-standard reliability.

However, human error does occur and advancements in medicine, psychotherapy, and the neurology of disorders are inevitable. While it is believed that the information contained in this book is accurate, neither the author or the publisher can warrant that the interventions offered are the only, the best, or most up-to-date ones available at the time of reading. Therefore, the author and publisher can accept no responsibility or liability for either the accuracy or the application of this knowledge.

Continue to be an educated agent. Particularly when dealing with drug abuse or chronic, debilitating and dangerous disorders. Readers should consult multiple sources before taking action. A response team which includes the teacher and student, an administrator, and mental-health professionals is typically the best option. When it comes to medications and treating serious disorders, always consult your physician.

Special Thanks to the following Chapter Reviewers:

Dr. Scott Hunter, The University of Chicago
Dr. Glen Rosen, Beth Israel Deaconess Hospital
Dr. Gordon Sherman, President, International Dyslexia Society
Dr. Robert Sapolsky, Stanford University

❖

*If a teacher keeps using
the same strategies over and over
and the student keeps failing,
who is really the slow learner?*

❖

TABLE OF CONTENTS

INTRODUCTION

Over the years I've enjoyed enthusiastic feedback from teachers who have used *Super Teaching* (1995) and *Teaching with the Brain in Mind* (1998). But the fact is, those books were written for the *majority* of students—those for whom simply smarter teaching strategies can make the difference. But what about the students who don't positively respond even in well-managed learning environments? I can't tell you how many times I've heard teachers ask, "But what about students who...?"

As I've said many times, healthy brains make healthy learners. And with healthy learners and a positive learning environment, you have a good shot at high achievement scores. But what happens when a learner is exposed to chronic stress, trauma, or drugs? What happens when a student's brain is impacted by developmental delays, abnormality, or chemical imbalances? Quite simply, you need better resources to succeed.

Different Brains, Different Learners is the first practical, comprehensive survey book that tells you in plain language how to recognize the most common conditions that challenge learners and how to help them succeed. While some learners will improve academically and behaviorally merely through your recognition, caring, and outreach, others will require therapeutic interventions and interdisciplinary care. In either case, there is hope. There are no "unreachables." And once you master these skills and strategies, your once "borderline" students can succeed. Isn't that what teaching is all about?

SPEECH AND LANGUAGE

Aphasia/Articulation Disorder
Expressive Language Disorder
Receptive Language Disorder
Auditory-Processing Deficit

BEHAVIORAL DISRUPTIONS

Attention-Deficit Disorder (ADD)
Oppositional Disorder (OPD)
Antisocial Disorder
Conduct Disorder

TOXINS

Malnutrition
Prenatal Toxins
Drugs
Environmental Toxins
Allergens

DEVELOPMENTAL

Autism
Delayed Development
William's Syndrome
Retardation

COMMON DISORDER GROUPS

ACADEMIC-SKILLS

Dyslexia
Other Reading Disorders
Writing Disorder
Arithmetic Disorder
Memory Disorders

MOTOR-SKILLS

Sensory Motor Deficits
Hypokinetic Disorders
Hyperactivity Disorders
Non-Verbal Learning Disabilities
Huntington's Disease
Cerebral Palsy
Ataxia

CONSCIOUSNESS

Epilepsy
Delayed Sleep
Schizophrenia

PERSONALITY DISORDERS

Addiction
Avoidant/Paranoid
Paranoid
Anorexia/Bulimia
Depression
Anxiety/Panic
Chronic Stress/Distress
Learned Helplessness

Disorders highlighted in blue are addressed in this book.

TEN TRUTHS
BEFORE YOU BEGIN

 There is **considerable comorbidity** (overlap) in these disorders. A single disorder is truly the exception. In this book, the disorders are singled out by chapter for the sake of convenience. Most commonly there are at least two, sometimes three, disorders present at the same time. Remember, everything in the brain is connected to something else.

 It's likely that **all of these disorders are multicausal**. Nevertheless, likely causes are listed separately in this book for the sake of clarity. Typically multiple factors—a genetic mutation or susceptibility, childhood neglect, toxins, malnutrition, abuse and/or prenatal trauma—are implicated. A traumatic life event or prolonged exposure to stress contributes to the problem.

 There are **multiple models** (and each accurate!) for understanding these disorders. Models come from the field of psychiatry, pediatric neurology, special education, and cutting-edge neuroscience. If you have a better or different model, that's okay, too. Over time, the most effective, least invasive models will rise to the surface.

 There is **no single location in the brain** for a disorder. The specific locations identified in this book rather offer a simple glimpse of some areas that are likely impacted. Nearly every neurological event is system-driven in ways that impact many areas of the brain. Remember, there are no isolated neurological events; instead, there are regulatory systems with identifiable pathways.

 There is no doubt **more to learn about these disorders**. Much greater study is needed. Brain-imaging technology is new and amazing, but it should never be the only source of information. Consider this resource as "Here's what we know so far."

6 Every learner can learn and improve. It's all a matter of resources (time, personnel, technology, medication, support, etc.). Make the commitment to ensure all students have a fighting chance.

7 Avoid perfectionism: It will rob you of the potential for gratifying rewards. Learn about one disorder at a time; and practice identifying specific learners. This book wasn't written in a day and you don't need to memorize it in a day to receive value from it. One chapter a week, or a month, is all you need. Just keep at it.

8 Look for students' strengths. Not every learner can become excellent in everything. There are significant genetic and environmental variations in the human species. Recent evidence suggests that the number of brain cells between students varies by more than 20 percent. The impact of this finding is mind-boggling.

9 Attitude and knowledge are equally important. Your belief in the highest possibilities of each learner and your capacity to identify symptoms and activate appropriate responses and resources are the most important variables in learner success.

10 Take pride in everyday successes—whether large or small. Learners learn much more from *who* you are than *what* you teach. Maybe your biggest gift is caring and doing your best. Never underestimate the power of hope or compassionate relationships, nor the value of implicit learning and positive role modeling.

Pre-Test:
Can You Identify These Learners?

(Go ahead and write in this book: you have the author's permission!)

LEARNER #1   "ASHLEY"

Symptoms

◆ Loses her temper often
◆ Argues with adults; defies authority and rejects adults' requests or rules; complies about 10 to 20 percent of the time
◆ Deliberately annoys others and is easily annoyed herself
◆ Blames others for her own mistakes or misbehavior
◆ Angry and resentful; vindictive for no apparent reason
◆ Swears and uses obscene language

Ashley is eight years old and smart. She's managed to get just about everyone in class mad at her. What's most likely going on? Answer:_____

LEARNER #2   "BRENT"

Symptoms

◆ Inattentive to others
◆ Easily distracted
◆ Engages in a lot of head turning to hear better
◆ Retrieval problems ("Um ....I forget the word")
◆ Difficulty following oral directions
◆ Omits word endings
◆ Speaks words out of order
◆ Mistaken words—says "starvation army" instead of Salvation Army or "fum" instead of thumb

This pattern began early, before he entered school. He's in the third grade, doing poorly, and he has not been tested. What's most likely going on? Answer:_____

LEARNER #3   "MICHELE"

Symptoms

◆ Decrease in energy
◆ Change in appetite and subsequent weight
◆ Feelings of worthlessness and guilt
◆ Inability to think clearly or concentrate; indecisiveness
◆ Thoughts of death, suicidal imaginings
◆ Persistent sad, anxious, or empty mood
◆ Feelings of hopelessness; pessimism
◆ Loss of interest or pleasure in ordinary activities or hobbies
◆ Restlessness, irritability, unexplained aches and pains
◆ Unusual loss of friends, reduction in academic performance

Michele is a fourth-grader who did well last year. This year her mother is being treated for cancer.
What's most likely going on? Answer:_____

LEARNER #4   "JASON"

Symptoms

◆ Rarely finishes his work
◆ Calls out answers in class; never waits his turn
◆ Easily and consistently distracted
◆ Exhibits weak follow-through and preparation for future events
◆ Wants everything right away; no patience
◆ Personal areas (desk) are a mess
◆ Doesn't seem able to reflect on the past to learn from it
◆ Doesn't sit still; always on the go
◆ Can't hold several thoughts at a time
◆ Hindsight or foresight rarely evident

Jason is a second-grade student with plenty of enthusiasm. He gets average grades.
What's most likely going on? Answer:_____

LEARNER #5 "LEE"

Symptoms

◆ Has trouble with sequencing, prioritizing, and completing tasks
◆ Takes spoken or written language literally
◆ Has difficulty following oral directions and remembering them
◆ Inability to rhyme by age four
◆ Confuses left and right, over and under, before and after, and other directionality words and concepts
◆ Lack of dominant handedness; switches hands between or even during tasks
◆ Unable to correctly complete phonemic awareness tasks
◆ Has difficulty learning the names and sounds of letters and writing them in alphabetical order

Lee, a seventh-grader, likes to read but struggles to maintain average grades. He rarely completes his assignments. What's most likely going on? Answer:_____

LEARNER #6 "JOSHUA"

Symptoms

◆ Inappropriate emotional outbursts with random acts of destruction
◆ Consistently hurtful towards peers—swatting, hitting, and verbal intimidation
◆ Refuses to follow directions directly; consistently challenges authority
◆ Loud and aggressive communication patterns, often taunting the teacher and using vulgar language
◆ Unwilling to participate with others in normal social activities
◆ Is prone to lie

This pattern began in first grade and has continued into high school.
What's most likely going on? Answer:_____

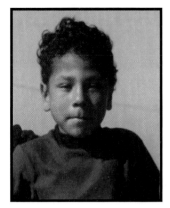

LEARNER #7   "MIGUEL"

Symptoms

◆ Difficulty structuring work time

◆ Impaired rates of learning and poor memory

◆ Has trouble generalizing behaviors and information

◆ Sometimes exhibits impulsive behavior

◆ Easily distracted and frequently exhibits reduced attention span

◆ Displays a sense of fearlessness and is unresponsive to verbal cautions

◆ Displays poor social judgment

◆ Has trouble internalizing modeled behaviors

◆ Language *production* is higher than *comprehension*

◆ Overall poor problem-solving strategies

◆ May have unusual facial features

Miguel has had these problems for years. In spite of this, he has been passed from one teacher to the next. What's most likely going on? Answer:_____

LEARNER #8   "COURTNEY"

Symptoms

◆ Displays a high level of apathy, listlessness, or lack of inertia

◆ Passive and unresponsive in spite of shocking or surprising events

◆ Does not initiate new activities or learning

◆ Does not feel in control of her environment; likely to say, "What's the point?" "Why bother?" "Who cares" or "So what?"

◆ Lack of hostility even when hostility is warranted

◆ Increased sarcasm

Courtney is twenty-one. She attends adult school because, if she doesn't, she will be kicked out of her house. The above symptoms have continued for about three to four months. Her teacher cannot quite nail down what's wrong. What's most likely going on? Answer:_____

LEARNER #9 "JEFFREY"

Symptoms

◆ Extreme fidgeting; stands instead of sits; walks instead of stands; and runs instead of walks

◆ Irritability and emotional immaturity

◆ Ignores routines and rules

◆ Exhibits continual action; does not use caution

◆ Constant tactile manipulation

◆ Often taps, touches, or pushes others

Jeffrey has exhibited this behavior pattern from a very early age. He seems to be on high power, while everyone else is operating at normal speed. What's most likely going on?

Answer:_____

LEARNER #10 "MARY"

Symptoms

◆ Seems to be edgy and on alert

◆ Trance-like state is common; doesn't "snap out of it" quickly

◆ Appears bored and disconnected

◆ Short-term memory loss and inability to prioritize

◆ Makes careless errors in her work

◆ Decreased social contact

◆ Doesn't remember "where" questions

◆ Loss of creativity and poor concentration

◆ Seems to be sick more often than peers

Mary, a high-school student, is struggling when, just a few years prior, she seemed so enthusiastic. Now it seems she is in a trance all the time. What's most likely going on?

Answer:_____

Each chapter addresses a different type of learner. Once you finish reading this book, quiz yourself again with the post-test. Meanwhile talk about the material, try it out, work with a study group, and really get it in your body. What you are about to learn will make a dramatic difference in your work. To find the answers to this quiz, continue reading.

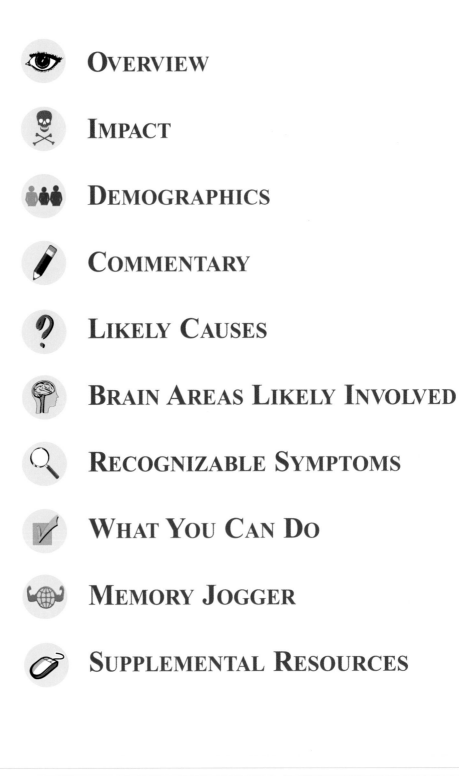

The Impulsive Learner:
Attention-Deficit Disorder

 ## OVERVIEW

Attention-Deficit Disorder (ADD) is the most commonly diagnosed behavioral disorder in students. The condition is characterized by impulsiveness and time disorientation. Earlier it was believed there were several strains of the disorder—for example, attention-deficit with hyperactivity and attention-deficit without hyperactivity. The current thinking is that hyperactivity is sometimes a common symptom of ADD, sometimes an age- or stage-related issue, and sometimes a behavior exhibited by highly tactile learners. In addition, current evidence suggests that ADD is not so much a problem of attention or skill, but of performance (i.e., impulse control). For example, Johnny may know what 5 x 3 is, but when asked to complete a problem on the chalk board, he may be unable to perform on the spot. Essentially, the student may be learning but cannot always be evaluated in the traditional sense. In ADD subjects the prefrontal cortex, the brain's "executive" area, is ineffective in the following functions:

▼ **Separating external (environmental) from internal (mental) states/stimulation**
▼ **Moving from other-directed to self-directed**
▼ **Distinguishing the present from the future**
▼ **Delaying immediate gratification**

The concept of time as a diagnostic tool is important to the understanding of Attention-Deficit Disorder. Sufferers typically have a "temporal myopia," meaning they are "nearsighted" to future problems/consequences. In other words, ADD sufferers do not plan for the future. This is not a pathology, but rather a dimensional trait. The greatest impairment is seen in the handling of daily responsibilities that require a sense of timing and restraint.

To fully understand and accurately diagnose Attention-Deficit Disorder, it is necessary to consider the age of the sufferer. In 4- and 5-year-olds, both inattention and hyperactivity are likely dominant symptoms; however, by age 6 or 7, the primary problem typically shifts to one of impulse control. Students with ADD may know what to do, but they are not always able to do it because of an inability to manage their own responses. This does not, however, mean they are not smart or not learning.

Criteria for Diagnosing ADD

1. The symptoms or behaviors appear before age 7.
2. The symptoms or behaviors last at least 6 months.
3. The level of disturbance is more severe and frequent than age norms.
4. The behaviors create a real handicap in at least two areas of the individual's life (i.e., school, home, social settings).

 # IMPACT

Since 1990, the total number of American students diagnosed with ADD has increased from 900,000 to approximately 7 million, and the use of stimulant medications (such as Ritalin) has increased 700 percent in the same period. Many students under the age of 4 are being diagnosed with ADD and 57 percent of them are taking at least one drug to treat it. As they grow, students with ADD are more at risk for anxiety, depression, and drug abuse. About 25 percent also have learning disabilities, and as many as 50 percent develop conduct problems. The condition can make life very difficult for families and teachers.

The prevailing therapy for ADD is drug therapy with stimulants such as Ritalin, Adderall, or Cylert. Some evidence, in fact, suggests that 80 percent of pediatric visits for ADD result in a stimulant prescription. Concern exists that this condition is both under diagnosed in some and over diagnosed in others—especially in children. Another concern is that behavioral therapy is not used as commonly as drug therapy. Many feel that the most effective treatment for children with ADD is (1) an accurate diagnosis; (2) a compatible/flexible environment; and (3) a combined treatment of medication and behavioral therapy, if necessary. Left untreated or misdiagnosed, ADD can have a long-term adverse impact on the child and their academic, social, and emotional well being.

Although researchers are still determining the effects of ADD in adults, most agree that through training, life adjustments, and accommodation, many individuals with ADD ultimately lead satisfying lives and successful careers.

DEMOGRAPHICS

ADD affects about 5 percent (estimates range from 2 to 10 percent) of American children and 15 to 20 million Americans of all ages. It impacts five times as many boys as girls and twice as many Caucasians as African Americans. Prescription medications are three times more likely to be used in the treatment of boys than girls, and, as children with ADD age, the use of medication increases. By the fifth grade, 19 to 20 percent of Caucasian boys were taking a medication for ADD, and some middle schools report as many as 50 percent.

Women with ADD report having more depressive episodes in their lives, lower self-esteem, more feelings of anxiety, higher levels of stress, and more frequent involvement in psychotherapy than women who don't have ADD. ADD sufferers also engage in less task-oriented and more emotional coping activities than non-ADD sufferers, and tend towards an external locus of control (i.e., they feel they have less control over their lives).

 # COMMENTARY

Comorbidity (or overlapping conditions) is common in ADD sufferers. In fact, some studies suggest that only 3 percent of sufferers over the course of their lifetime have ADD alone. Conversely, about 56 percent of ADD sufferers have four or more psychiatric comorbidities throughout their lifetime. About 11 percent of ADD sufferers experience one other psychiatric condition and 18 percent have three. Men with ADD experience higher rates of Conduct Disorder, Antisocial Personality Disorder, alcohol and drug dependence, and stuttering than women. But, women with ADD experience higher rates of depression, Bulimia Nervosa, and simple phobias. Because of this high rate of comorbidity, the risk for misdiagnosis and undiscovered problems is high.

SPECT SCANS REVEAL DIFFERENCES BETWEEN NON-MEDICATED AND MEDICATED ADD BRAIN

Undersurface SPECT view of ADD brain at rest. Note lessened activity (see dark "holes") in top prefrontal area—the area needed for focus.

Undersurface SPECT view of ADD brain after treatment with the stimulant Adderall. Note increased activity in upper (prefrontal) area

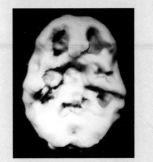 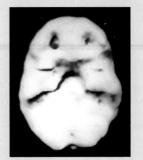

Source: *Images into Human Behavior: A Brain SPECT Atlas*, Daniel G. Amen, MD, 2000

While ADD does not cause Conduct Disorder or violent behavior, it is correlated with negative conduct. The crux of the problem is that ADD patients are often given medications without the social interventions to support positive behavioral change. Students who "act out" are typically perceived and treated differently by adults, which impacts environment, and ultimately changes everyone's responses in "the loop."

This viscous cycle feeds the student's feelings of anger, inadequacy, and abnormality, thereby increasing the risk of substance abuse. A disconcerting statistic reveals that as many as 65 percent of children with ADD will develop dysfunctional social behaviors and conditions, the most common of which is Oppositional Disorder. When ADD is left untreated, the condition is more likely to worsen and be complicated with comorbid psychiatric conditions. Although ADD represents a serious challenge to classroom teachers, the condition itself can be effectively treated.

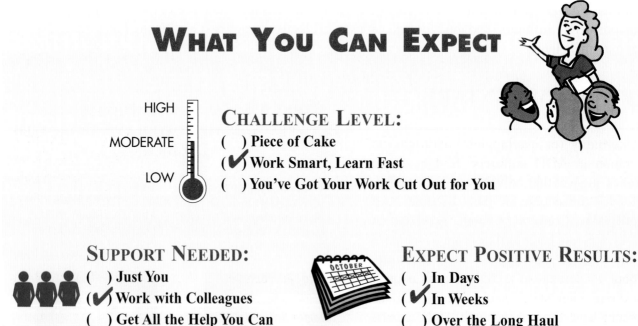

WHAT YOU CAN EXPECT

HIGH
MODERATE
LOW

CHALLENGE LEVEL:
( ) Piece of Cake
(✔) Work Smart, Learn Fast
( ) You've Got Your Work Cut Out for You

SUPPORT NEEDED:
( ) Just You
(✔) Work with Colleagues
( ) Get All the Help You Can

EXPECT POSITIVE RESULTS:
( ) In Days
(✔) In Weeks
( ) Over the Long Haul

? LIKELY CAUSES

A single clear cause of ADD has not been identified. We do know, however, that it is not caused by poor parenting, too much television, or poor diet. These factors may exacerbate ADD, but they do not cause the condition. Genetic and environmental factors are presently being explored.

Heredity

Genetic researchers in five different studies have discovered a link between a particular gene called the DRD4 repeater gene and ADD. These studies suggest that up to 80 percent of the variance in the trait is now thought to be genetically based. Their work has shown that some students may inherit a biochemical condition that influences the expression of ADD symptoms.

Physiology

Recently, scientists have found that specific areas in the frontal lobe and basal ganglia of ADD patients show a reduction in both size and activity of about 10 percent.

Chemical Dysregulation

Some ADD research has implicated the neurotransmitter dopamine. Dopamine pathways in the brain, which link the basal ganglia and prefrontal cortex (PFC), appear to play a major role in ADD. Insufficient "fuel or stimulation" in the PFC prevents this part of the brain from playing its standard impulse-regulation role. However, since antidepressants are often successful in treating ADD, misdiagnosis and/or serotonin involvement questions are also raised.

Head Injury

Although the skull is hard, the brain is soft, and upon impact, can be launched into its hard casing, making it very susceptible to damage. The typical growing-up experience presents countless possibilities for injury: a fall from a bike, bunk-bed, tree, or roof, a car accident, a sports injury, a fight, or physical abuse. Every one of these incidents can put a student at risk for developing learning and conduct problems later on. Why? The area that regulates impulse control, the prefrontal cortex, is the area of the brain most easily damaged.

Frontal-Lobe Symmetry

Some ADD research has implicated over-symmetry between the left and right frontal lobes in the brain. In general, the left frontal lobe is more involved with approach behaviors and the right frontal lobe with

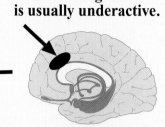

ADD AND THE BRAIN

Prefrontal cortex has lower activity level compared to normal.

Anterior cingulate is usually underactive.

These are the pathways used by the neurotransmitter norepinephrine to boost activity and enhance the signal-to-noise ratio.

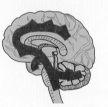

avoidance behaviors. In normal subjects, the right frontal lobe is a bit larger than the left, which would seem to indicate a stronger tendency towards avoiding negative repercussions (or stronger impulse control).

Other Potential Risk Factors

Additional risk factors include a family history of alcoholism, female relatives that have Briquet's Syndrome (hysteria/imagined illness), living in poverty, being male, and severe family relationship problems such as a nasty divorce, abuse, or neglect. Retardation, Conduct Disorder, prenatal smoking, and low birth weight can also increase the risk.

BRAIN AREAS LIKELY INVOLVED

Prefrontal Cortex

The most common symptoms of ADD are all associated with the frontal lobes and/or prefrontal cortex. These symptoms include lack of impulse control, critical learning from experience, and perseverance, as well as disorganization, poor self-monitoring, and weak social skills.

Blood Flow and Brain Activity

Some research has implicated under-arousal of the central nervous system in ADD. As evidenced by PET scans, normalization occurs when the subjects are given stimulants to increase blood flow. Such an intervention also typically reduces the flow of dopamine to the frontal lobes—facilitating normal function.

Recognizable Symptoms

An effective instrument for a comprehensive evaluation of ADD has yet to be designed. Presently, a diagnostician evaluates the presence of co-existing medical or educationally-disabling conditions, and excludes alternative explanations for behavioral and academic problems. Start by observing behavior patterns and listening for background information.

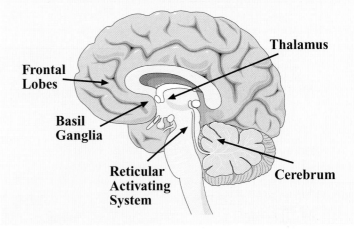

BRAIN AREAS INVOLVED IN REGULATING ATTENTION AND IMPULSIVITY

Thalamus
Frontal Lobes
Basil Ganglia
Reticular Activating System
Cerebrum

Behaviors That May Provide Clues to ADD

▼ Poor mental calculation skills
▼ Skills highly variable
▼ Poor planning for future events; weak preparation skills
▼ Insensitive to errors
▼ Rarely finishes work
▼ Calls out answers in class; rarely waits turn
▼ Frequent distraction

▼ Impaired sense of time passage
▼ No patience; wants everything right now
▼ Messy desk or personal space
▼ Inability to reflect on the past and learn from it
▼ Can't sit still; always moving or fidgeting
▼ Limited short-term memory
▼ Lack of foresight or hindsight

Ironically, students with ADD can be very smart. Teaching them the basic skills alone, however, is not enough. They need to be taught with a gentle approach *how* to recognize and manage their impulses appropriately and *when* and *where* to apply newly learned skills.

A COMPREHENSIVE ADD ASSESSMENT INCLUDES:

▼ A complete family history, including medical, psychological, academic, and emotional/social functioning
▼ Interviews with significant others
▼ Observation over time to understand the depth and scope of the condition
▼ Observation in natural settings, not just in the assessor's office
▼ Use of a rating scale to capture the degree of impairment
▼ Intelligence testing (sometimes included)
▼ Assessment of developmental abilities, attention span, and impulsivity

A complete assessment is usually best conducted by a developmental pediatrician, a pediatric neurologist, or a psychiatrist in conjunction with a qualified psychologist.

 # WHAT YOU CAN DO

ADD should be taken seriously. It is not a myth, but it is not an urgent, threatening menace either. The condition is treatable. If ignored, however, more serious problems are bound to follow. ADD sufferers are at high risk for academic and social failure, consequences that can be avoided with proper intervention. Since ADD frequently coexists with other problems, diagnosis is sometimes tricky. Vision and/or hearing problems need to be ruled out first. Students with ADD frequently have a specific learning disability, as well. They may have trouble mastering language, reading, math, or performing handwriting. Focus on the ADD student's strengths and provide extra support wherever needed.

Trying to fix or cure the ADD student is counterproductive. They are not broken; rather, they need understanding and accommodation. Although ADD is not always considered a learning disability, its interference with concentration and attention make it very difficult to perform well in school. More serious perhaps, is the fact that many boys with ADD also have Oppositional Disorder. These students can be very stubborn, belligerent, and have frequent angry outbursts that make them difficult to manage in class. ADD can also progress to the more serious condition, Conduct Disorder. Students with this combination of problems may fall into serious legal trouble; they may steal, set fires, destroy property, or act out violently; they may act recklessly and take undue risks. A student who exhibits these antisocial behaviors should be promptly referred to the school psychologist or other medical/mental-health professional.

As an Educator

Many experienced educators, by virtue of necessity, have learned to accommodate the ADD learner. What do they do? First and foremost, they maintain a positive attitude ("I like ADD learners; they have more energy and enthusiasm!"). They also have learned to tweak the balance between control/direction and student empowerment, and to identify the difference between ADD and ADD combined with other more serious disorders. Lastly, when they are in "over their head," they make the appropriate referral. The accommodations you learn to make for the ADD learner also benefit the rest of your students. Managing ADD effectively requires good basic teaching skills.

Provide Accommodation

Understanding the condition and accommodating the ADD student are essential. If you are a new teacher, the challenge will be greater, as you'll have more on your plate and your stress level may be higher. But remember, the best way to manage ADD students effectively is to provide a positive learning environment that focuses on their strengths, rather than their weaknesses. Be flexible, but maintain consistent boundaries on important issues, such as those that involve their own and others' safety.

Refer Out as Necessary

If you suspect the ADD student may have a comorbid condition, promptly refer them to the school psychologist and/or other medical/mental-health professional. This is your call and it's an important one. Ask yourself, "Can I handle this student? Am I skilled enough? Is the student otherwise healthy and happy?" If the answers are yes, the following list of strategies may be enough to manage the ADD student without intervention. If, however, the answer to any of these questions is no, then seek appropriate help.

Use a Behavioral Modification Approach

Focus on reinforcing positive behaviors and rechanneling negative ones (see "Parent/Teacher Tips for Reinforcing Positive Behaviors" on page 12). Behavior modification is most effective when done immediately at the time the behavior occurs. If you attend to it later, the students aren't likely to internalize the information. Obviously, you can't always be at the ADD student's side, but create an infrastructure that supports them as much as possible (i.e., star charts, extra privileges, self-checklists, cooperative teams, partner grading, numerous feedback mechanisms, etc.). Pinpoint one or two behaviors to focus on at a time, so that the student (and you) don't get too overwhelmed and tired. Choose your battles carefully.

Avoid Threats/Distress

Too much pressure causes the ADD brain to shut down and underperform. This is why a gentle and moderate approach is best. Rather than making threats like "If you don't stop talking, you're going to have to stay after school," say "Let's set three goals that we want to accomplish today." In five minutes, I'll check back with you to see if you're on track." You never want to embarrass a student for his/her ADD behavior. It is not by choice: They have a disorder. These students are different, but then again, aren't we all in one way or another?

Provide External Reinforcers

Since the ADD student has a much harder time with delaying gratification than the average student, provide plenty of external motivators. Good motivation tools include a point system, a star chart, peer approval, extra recognition, responsibilities, and/or privileges. Acknowledge progress, appropriate behaviors, and goal achievement. Encourage parents to use similar motivators.

Establish Routines

Create high predictability through daily and weekly events that always happen on cue. For example, provide a daily overview of the lesson plan; open class the same way each time; transition from one activity to the next in a routine way; end class with a predictable closure; and make one or more days out of the week special in some way (i.e., Monday "Goal Setting" Session, Wednesday "Check-In" Session, and Friday "Celebration"). When the routine varies, acknowledge the change.

Incorporate More Movement

Include plenty of movement and hands-on activities in your lesson planning. Vary the types of movements from sitting to standing to walking to running. To control inappropriate behavior, limit "free" time. Establish a signal system that the ADD student understands so that communication with him/her can be either verbal or non-verbal. A signal should be agreed upon to indicate to the student that it's time for them to take a walk once around the building. Make sure that they know you expect them back within five minutes.

Sharpen Communication

Important information such as ground rules, grading policies, team/group divisions, upcoming events, etc. should be written down and posted in obvious locations in the room. Make it as easy as possible for the ADD learner to access information. Keep oral instructions brief and repeat them; provide written instructions (and review them orally) for multi-step processes; and divide learning tasks and homework into steps.

Manage Information Flow

Teach learners how to manage information so that they don't become overwhelmed. Show them how to scan and review reading material, how to focus on first and last sentences and paragraphs, and how to break tasks into chunks. Provide helpful self-check criteria and/or daily checklists; show them how to proof their work before turning it in; help them set up a planning calendar or notebook (i.e., listing homework assignments and due dates; textbooks/supplies needed, etc.). Write instructions out for them, and repeat important information. Teach them memory tricks (mnemonics) like writing key words in the air and associating something they want to remember with a silly or novel visual image.

Increase Feedback

Focus on the student's strengths and successes. Acknowledge even partial progress. Don't wait until mastery is achieved to praise them. Use external motivators like progress charts and point systems, in which good behavior earns points towards classroom privileges. Make a practice of "catching the ADD student being good." Incorporate group activities to increase peer feedback.

Teach Time-Management Skills

Teach students how to break up learning tasks into chunks and manage them with an external reminder system (i.e., planning calendar, notes, computer programs, etc.). Help the student manage their time in the classroom with prompts, pointers, timers, bells, and timekeepers. Be sure to allot time expectations to assignments so that there are no surprises. Provide ample warning when a transition from one activity to another is about to occur. A buddy system can sometimes reduce impulse-control problems and provide additional support for the ADD student.

Functionalize Classroom Space

Consider creating stations in the classroom for various functions—for example, where students can go to read or write without distraction, listen to soothing music, or engage in hands-on activities. At the very least, provide a cozy "student office" space where working quietly and independently is encouraged. Room dividers, storage cabinets, bookcases, or simple plastic boxes can be easily adapted for this purpose.

Involve Entire Class

Hold class meetings and address behavior topics that are especially relevant to ADD, such as respect, breaking bad habits, problem solving, noise levels, etc., Be careful, however, not to single out ADD students. You might introduce a topic or theme each Monday that will be addressed throughout the week. Facilitate a discussion about how it feels to be disrespected, interrupted, or bullied by others. To be maximally effective, introduce only one topic at a time.

Recommend Behavioral Therapy

Just because a student is on Ritalin or Adderall does not mean the ADD has been effectively treated. Students who get behavioral therapy in conjunction with medication usually best adapt to the classroom culture.

PARENT/TEACHER TIPS FOR REINFORCING POSITIVE BEHAVIORS

✓ Focus on the child's strengths; give credit even when only partially due.

✓ Avoid arguing and no-win discussions.

✓ Set fair limits and stick to them; no negotiating.

✓ Avoid punishment or taking away privileges as the primary reinforcement; use positive discipline/reinforcement methods as much as possible.

✓ Role model healthy behaviors; be organized yourself; avoid using substances for coping with stress; get enough sleep, recreation, and exercise.

✓ Walk your students through complex tasks, dividing them into manageable steps.

✓ Avoid unrealistic expectations (i.e., that he/she should be able to remember a five-step sequence).

✓ Develop your contingency-management skills; always have a plan A, B, and C, and remain flexible and calm when faced with the unexpected.

✓ Maintain clear daily, weekly, and monthly goals; help learners create their own personal goals, as well.

✓ Always use a loving approach in spite of your frustrations.

✓ Encourage healthy peer relationships; provide guidance on how to be a good friend to others.

✓ Celebrate appropriately when a performance goal is reached.

As a Parent

Having a child with Attention-Deficit Disorder can clearly be a frustrating experience for parents, making it even more important to keep the big picture in mind. Be sure your child knows that he or she is loved and valued despite his or her condition. Does this mean we should overlook inappropriate behaviors? No. Rather, guide them gently and patiently towards a clear goal. In the process, make sure you instill in them the following:

1. A sense that they have some control over their own lives.
2. A sense that what they do is different from who they are.
3. A feeling that they are loved despite their condition.

Gather Information

If you suspect your child may have ADD, begin to gather information. Consider the following questions in determining whether to have your child professionally assessed by a physician, psychologist, or other mental-health specialist:

1. Are the troubling behaviors excessive and pervasive? Do they occur more often than peer norms?
2. Are the troubling behaviors chronic, not just a response to a temporary situation?
3. Do the troubling behaviors occur in several settings, not just at school or at home?

If the answers to these questions are yes, a professional assessment is recommended.

Consult a Physician/Mental-Health Professional

If your family doctor does not impress you as being knowledgeable on the subject, consider taking your child to a developmental pediatrician or a psychologist that specializes in learning disabilities. Psychostimulants such as Ritalin (methylphenidate) and Dexedrine (dextroamphetamine), as well as some antidepressants, are the most widely accepted medications for ADD. Many psychiatrists now prefer the stimulant Adderall, since it has proven in some studies to be more effective than Ritalin. However, no single ADD drug always works for every child, and doctors depend on the input of parents and teachers for finding the most effective treatment for the individual. Sometimes a series of drugs must be tried before a child's behavior improves, and side effects are always a serious consideration.

Consider the Value of Brain Scans

Today it is not uncommon for parents to request a brain scan to confirm an ADD diagnosis. Both PET and SPECT scans clearly show the areas of the brain that are metabolically underactive or overactive. However, such tests are expensive ($1200-$3200) and are not always covered by health insurance. Altropane, an imaging agent developed by Boston Life Sciences, Inc., is another potentially valuable tool for confirming an ADD diagnosis; however, it will not be on the market until 2002.

Brain scans show a contrast between two states—resting and concentration. Normally when a person thinks out a problem or engages in an intellectual task, increased activity occurs in the area of the brain responsible for that function. However, when the ADD brain is challenged by a task that requires concentration, we see the opposite happen—brain activity actually decreases. The harder the student tries, the more the activity decreases. Brain scans, thus, provide concrete physical evidence of the condition. If the diagnosis is positive, and ADD is confirmed, do not ignore it. There are a number of good options available for treating the disorder.

Prepare Your Child for School

Most students with ADD do better in school once they are on an effective medication combined with behavioral therapy. Behavioral therapy alone, however, is not optimally effective in treating severe ADD behaviors/symptoms. Before your child gets caught up in a negative cycle at school, provide extra preparation for their entry into the school environment.

HOW TO PREPARE THE ADD CHILD FOR SCHOOL

✓ Design a personalized behavior program: Target a few unacceptable behaviors with clear, consistent consequences that are fully understood and agreed upon by your child. Consequences should *not* be humiliating, threatening, or physically violent (i.e., spanking).

✓ Role model effective organizational skills: Encourage the older children to use planning techniques, such as a daily planner, computer software program, or a simple notebook.

✓ Modify the environment: Request that your child be able to sit near the front of the classroom; they need plenty of time to engage in tactile stimulation and manipulation activities; allow them to stand instead of sit, etc.

✓ Reinforce self-esteem: Encourage mastery in your child's areas of strength and personal interest; provide plenty of feedback and positive reinforcement.

✓ Encourage active learning: Use visual aids, hands-on experiences, and group processes when possible to engage them. Teach them study skills, such as reading with a highlighter (underlining), active listening (note taking), reading for detail, summarizing, and memory "tricks" such as subvocalizing (whispering) as a memory aid.

✓ Repeat and Remind: Repeat important information a number of times. Remind your child to consult their notebooks and planning calendars at the end of the day to ensure they bring home the necessary supplies for their homework assignment.

✓ Be consistent about homework expectations.

Cooperate with School Personnel

Talk to your child's teacher; try to get a clear picture of their experience level and philosophical approach with regards to ADD. If you wish to get more information or are concerned that the teacher is not able to work with your child effectively, consult with the school nurse, school psychologist, or principal if necessary. Be sure that school personnel know what medication (if any) your child is taking, and inform them of the approach you're using at home so that it can be reinforced at school. Agree on appropriate rules and consequences.

Consider Diet/Nutritional Supplements

A high-protein/low-carbohydrate diet is best for ADD sufferers as excess carbohydrates can negatively impact dopamine levels. The high-protein/low-carbohydrate combination also helps stabilize blood-sugar levels. Tyrosine and Ginko Biloba supplements can help increase blood flow and activity in the frontal-lobes, the brain area most implicated in ADD. Tyrosine (children: 250mg 2 times/day; adults: 1000mg 2 times/day) is especially effective when ADD symptoms are  mild. It's also a good idea to support your child's healthy diet of whole foods with a high quality multi-vitamin/mineral supplement taken first thing in the morning on an empty stomach. In addition, grape seed extract has been found to be helpful in some case studies, though a large-scale study has yet to be conducted.

While it is true than there are clear links between dietary consumption and behaviors, pinpointing particular reactions will probably require the assistance of a professional nutritionist. Many potential food allergies exist that could exacerbate the problem. Some parents claim that a diet low in sugar and high in complex carbohydrates (versus simple ones) and high in protein with plenty of fruits and vegetables has benefited their ADD child. Dietary approaches such as these, although appealing, have not been *proven* effective in therapeutic trials. This, however, is not to say that they don't help.

Employ Biofeedback

Some sufferers are helped by alternative therapeutic approaches, such as biofeedback. Biofeedback is a treatment activity that uses simple EEG instruments to measure bodily reactions (like pulse rate, breathing, or sweating) while the patient performs particular tasks. The information, fed back to the patient, provides helpful feedback for affecting change. For example, while trying to match up items on a computer screen, they can see how their anxiety level increases the harder they try. With practice, they can learn to consciously slow down their breathing, heart rate, etc. This can help the ADD sufferer calm down and approach problem solving more effectively. While some controversy about the effectiveness of biofeedback exists, when it is facilitated by a skilled professional, some learners have experienced success at retraining their frontal lobes, thereby, decreasing impulsivity and increasing concentration.

 # MEMORY JOGGER

Remember this face? This is "Jason," one of the learners introduced in the pre-test at the front of the book. He's also the student who fits the profile for Attention-Deficit Disorder. Like the others, Jason is unique—he exhibits a pattern of symptoms that are associated with a specific disorder. However, some of these symptoms can be observed in other conditions as well. This is why you want to look for *patterns* rather than *isolated behaviors*. To help you remember what's important in assessing ADD, take a moment, relax, and focus on the photo, the symptoms, and the key points of this chapter.

Symptoms
- Rarely finishes his work
- Calls out answers in class; never waits his turn
- Easily and consistently distracted
- Exhibits weak follow-through and preparation for future events
- Wants everything right away; no patience
- Personal areas (desk) are a mess
- Doesn't seem able to reflect on the past to learn from it
- Doesn't sit still; always on the go
- Can't hold several thoughts at a time
- Hindsight or foresight rarely evident

SUPPLEMENTAL RESOURCES

Books

Ritalin-Free Kids, by Judyth and Robert Ullman
The ADD/ADHD Checklist, by Sandra Rief
All About ADHD, by Linda Pfiffner
Taking Charge of AD/HD: The Authoritative Guide, by Russell Barkley
How to Reach and Teach ADD/ADHD Children, by Sandra Rief
The ADD/ADHD Behavior Change Resource Kit, by Grad Flick
Your Defiant Child: 8 Steps to Better Behavior, by Russell Barkley

Websites

www.cdc.gov *(Centers for Disease Control and Prevention)*
www.chadd.org *(Children and Adults with Attention-Deficit Disorder)*
www.ADD.org *(National Attention-Deficit Disorder Association)*
www.nih.gov *(National Institutes of Health)*

Organizations

Children and Adults with ADD (CHADD)
Contact: Jennifer Garner, 301-306-7070, ext. 102

from our parents. These styles are important because they shape our beliefs, which drive our actions, which impact our success in life.

The consistent theme here is *control*. When learners perceive they have *no control* over troubling experiences, learned helplessness is likely to develop. When students learn they do, however, *have control* over their thoughts and actions, they become proactive, persistent, resourceful, and ultimately, immune to learned helplessness. Thus, you can contribute immensely to the prevention and reversal of learned helplessness by empowering students more and controlling them less.

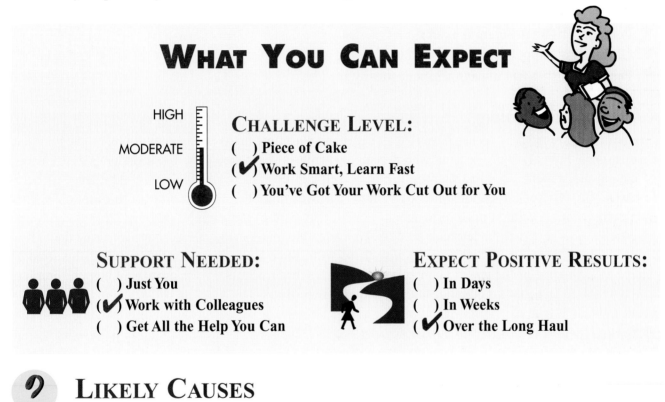

WHAT YOU CAN EXPECT

HIGH

MODERATE

LOW

CHALLENGE LEVEL:
( ) Piece of Cake
(✔) Work Smart, Learn Fast
( ) You've Got Your Work Cut Out for You

SUPPORT NEEDED:
( ) Just You
(✔) Work with Colleagues
( ) Get All the Help You Can

EXPECT POSITIVE RESULTS:
( ) In Days
( ) In Weeks
(✔) Over the Long Haul

❓ LIKELY CAUSES

The risk of learned helplessness varies significantly among people since perception plays a key role in the condition.

Neglect/Negative Role Modeling
Neglect of any kind, especially during the first few years of life, creates fertile ground for LH to take hold. Beyond this, if a child is surrounded by caretakers who feel "helpless," the risk of becoming "helpless"

themselves is much higher (i.e., as is sometimes reflected in multi-generation welfare families). Therefore, some would say LH is "contagious."

Trauma-Induced 'Debilitation'

It is possible for LH to be induced by a traumatic experience when all three of the following conditions are present: (1) intense negative experience; (2) a perceived lack of control during the trauma; and (3) the sufferer, at some point, decides to stop trying and forms a paralyzing belief. Paralyzing beliefs can be categorized as follows:

▼ **Personal ("The problem is me.")**
▼ **Global ("It happens in all areas of my life.")**
▼ **Permanent ("It will always happen, so why try?")**

Unconscious Enabling

Teachers (or parents) who do *too* much for students can over time inadvertently reinforce, or even induce, helplessness. For example, a teacher who repeatedly brings a sharpened pencil to a student's desk instead of having the student get up to sharpen it him/herself can unconsciously fuel the child's sense of helplessness. The teacher's intentions may be benign, but over time, the child can begin to question his/her own competency. Children need to be taught how to take care of themselves, and that struggle and mistakes are a natural part of the learning process. Well-meaning parents may think they are saving their child from "failure" by *doing*, rather than *helping* them with, their homework, but the result of this kind of "help" is a removal of the natural consequences and feedback necessary for growth. When children are overly-guarded from failure, they develop an intense fear of it.

Internalized/Externalized Oppression

Learned helplessness tends to take hold in individuals who mistakenly attribute their failures to a character defect (i.e., "I'm just stupid."). Along this line of thinking, a child who overhears a teacher or parent say they are "lazy" or "incapable" or "behind their classmates" in a subject may internalize the comment to the degree that it becomes a self-fulfilling prophecy. Some LH sufferers, on the other hand, experience the opposite distortion: They blame their failures on others, or the "bad" school, or the world as a whole. As a result they have given up any sense of control.

This tendency towards distorted thinking may, ultimately, be what determines an individual's susceptibility to learned helplessness. As depicted in the following illustration, the circular path from our thoughts to our behaviors is pretty clearcut. Our experiences shape our expectations and explanations, which shape our beliefs and reinforce our mental states, which, in turn, regulate our feelings of worthiness, competence, and potency, and ultimately impact our actions and responses to the world. Once a distortion takes hold, we inadvertently reinforce our original experience until the cycle is broken.

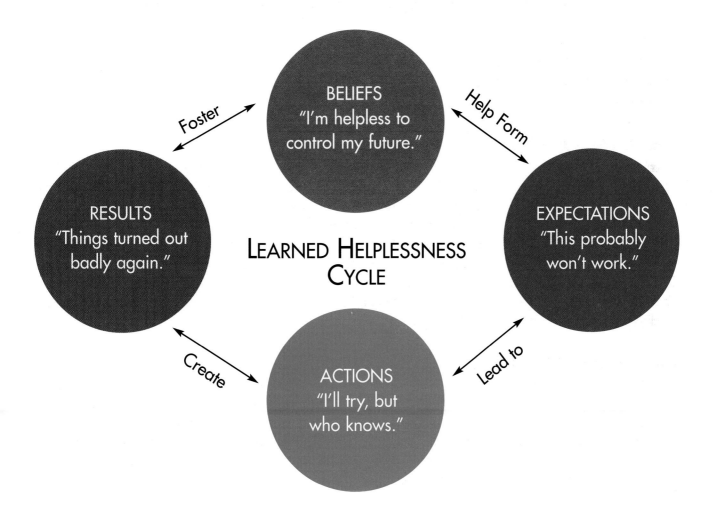

LEARNED HELPLESSNESS CYCLE

BELIEFS
"I'm helpless to control my future."

EXPECTATIONS
"This probably won't work."

RESULTS
"Things turned out badly again."

ACTIONS
"I'll try, but who knows."

Foster

Help Form

Lead to

Create

BRAIN AREAS LIKELY INVOLVED

Genes

Although there are no examples of human genetic models for learned helplessness, behaviors associated with the condition have been successfully bred in rats. Thus, a genetic model of human depression and/or anxiety (with implications for learned helplessness) is being investigated.

Frontal Lobes

Decisions are made in the medial-frontal cortex. In humans, there are multiple brain sights involved in LH, but these sites do not create the disorder; rather, they are always "present at the scene of the crime." While the biological substrates evident in LH may influence the disorder, it is the perceived absence of control, a psychological factor, that is key to its development. However, the variable of control does have significant biological consequences.

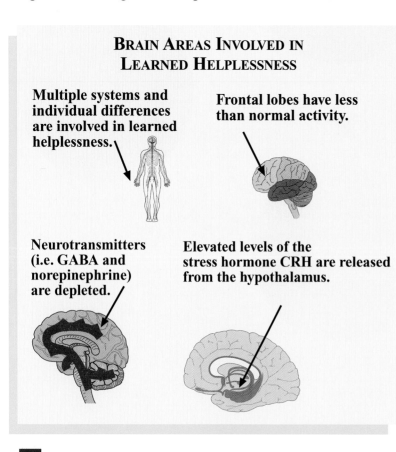

BRAIN AREAS INVOLVED IN LEARNED HELPLESSNESS

Multiple systems and individual differences are involved in learned helplessness.

Frontal lobes have less than normal activity.

Neurotransmitters (i.e. GABA and norepinephrine) are depleted.

Elevated levels of the stress hormone CRH are released from the hypothalamus.

Neurotransmitter Levels

Evidence suggests that chronic depletion of norepinephrine is evident in LH subjects. Produced in the locus ceruleus at the top of the brainstem and spreading to all areas of the brain, this neurotransmitter influences mood, arousal, and memory. Chronic depletions of gamma aminobutyric acid (GABA) and serotonin (mood regulator) have been found in LH sufferers, in addition to elevated analgesic (opiate) levels.

Hypothalamus

Corticotrophin release (CRF) hormones are manufactured by the paraventricular nucleus of the hypothalamus. These stress-response chemicals are present in higher levels after a LH episode.

RECOGNIZABLE SYMPTOMS

Learned helplessness can be easily confused with other conditions such as sleep disorders, stress disorders, fatigue, boredom, and depression. Therefore, it is important to pay close attention. Observe the student over a period of time and record what you see in a notebook or journal, if possible. The symptoms common to learned helplessness include the following:

▼ **Apathy and inertia**
▼ **Diminished response initiation** *(unresponsive to shocking events)*
▼ **Perceived lack of control over environment and circumstances**
▼ **Lack of assertiveness**
▼ **Lack of hostility when it is warranted**
▼ **Lack of motivation**
▼ **Increased sarcasm**
▼ **Statements of powerlessness** *(What's the point? Why bother? Who cares? So what?)*
▼ **Automaton-like behaviors** *(going through the motions)*
▼ **Cognition problems**
▼ **Loss of appetite and weight**

☑ WHAT YOU CAN DO

Fortunately, the effects of LH typically diminish over time aided by the normal day-to-day circumstances, responsibilities, emergencies, and developmental stages of life. Nevertheless, it is important to intervene on the student's behalf with effective classroom strategies as soon as you notice the symptoms of LH.

If, however, you suspect the more serious disorder, depression (which shares some LH symptoms), the student needs to be referred to the school psychologist (at the very least) immediately. In both conditions, the student may be passive, unwilling to participate, and "down," but the depressive's perception of the disorder is personal: "I'm the problem, and I'm no good; therefore, things will turn out badly." Conversely, the LH student perceives the problem as circumstantial: "Whatever I do I can't change the situation, so it doesn't matter. I can't change anything, so why try?"

Decreased Activity in Brains of Depressed and LH Patients

Note "holes" showing decreased activity at the top (frontal lobes) as well as elsewhere. The first two SPECT scans show the brain of a depressed patient that is similar to the deactivation patterns in the brain of a patient with learned helplessness.
The third scan is a healthy patient in a resting state showing smooth activations across the lobes.

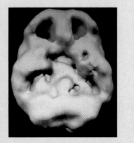 

Subjects with Depression/
Learned Helplessness

Subject with
healthy brain

Source: I*mages into Human Behavior: A Brain SPECT Atlas,*
Daniel G. Amen, MD, 2000

Due to the serious implications of depression (i.e., the risk of suicide), depressed individuals should receive professional therapeutic treatment without delay. The LH student, however, can usually be aided by a competent teacher with the help of sensitive parents without therapeutic intervention. With a good solid program that ensures small steps towards success, LH can be alleviated within a few weeks or months.

As an Educator

It is not uncommon for parents to blame LH on the school or teachers. This line of thinking, however, clearly stalls progress and can be extremely frustrating for conscientious teachers who understand the deeper implications of the condition. Learned helplessness can be the result of a single traumatic incident or developed over time. The root of the condition is a feeling of powerlessness and a debilitating belief that what you do simply doesn't matter. Certainly, institutions that inadvertently condition students to fail contribute to the incidence of learned helplessness. This speaks to the importance of hiring effective teachers and administrators who reinforce optimistic thinking and appropriate learner control. Administrators who empower their teachers ultimately empower their students.

TEACHER TIPS FOR PREVENTING AND ADDRESSING LEARNED HELPLESSNESS

✓ Recognize that the student is not to blame for his or her condition.

✓ Deepen your relationship with the student.

✓ Emphasize what a difference each student makes in class and in life.

✓ Encourage strong social relationships with peers through group work and cooperative learning experiences.

✓ Provide students with a greater sense of personal control by allowing them to make more choices between appropriate options.

✓ Encourage students to record their thoughts and feelings in a journal. Allow time for sharing them with peers (with the students' permission).

✓ Increase the amount of movement and hands-on activities in class.

✓ Encourage student involvement in theater, dance, art, or music.

✓ Play games and relays which encourage everyone's participation.

✓ Encourage students to enter an immersion or adventure program like Super Camp or Outward Bound. Encourage involvement in community service projects or after-school activities such as sports or social clubs.

✓ Provide an opportunity for students to begin taking care of a companion animal.

✓ Include parents in discussions about the issue.

✓ Provide a road map that outlines each day's activities so students know what to expect and can make smooth transitions from one activity to the next.

✓ Maintain optimism. You do make a difference.

It is essential to create a highly engaging atmosphere where students are encouraged to stay active, relate to others, and reflect on their learning. It may take some time to "rewire" the brain of the LH student, so don't get discouraged. The student didn't get this way over night, and they're not going to completely recover over night. However, with a consistent approach that ensures multiple small successes throughout the learning unit, the LH student will begin to show substantial progress.

As a Parent

Parents can help prevent or reverse LH by reinforcing responsible decision-making, an optimistic attitude, and a trial-and-error approach when faced with a challenge. Encourage your child to participate in activities he/she likes; validate small steps of progress; and provide support when challenged by a particular task or situation.

Do not mistake inertia for laziness. Lecturing the LH child is not the answer. Does this mean you should overlook inappropriate behaviors? No, but the LH child needs to feel loved and valued in spite of his/her challenges. Provide clear consistent boundaries and expectations with reasonable consequences for inappropriate behaviors. Foster a sense that what your child does is different from who they are.

Consider Psychotherapy

One form of psychotherapy, called cognitive therapy, has proven especially effective in addressing learned helplessness. In this modality, the client learns to identify automatic, negative thoughts and convert them into positive alternatives for viewing a problem. You might say that cognitive therapy teaches children to be "thought detectives." As they become more aware of their thoughts and feelings in particular situations, they observe how distortion can occur. As a parent, you can reinforce the idea that distortion intensifies the problem of LH. Ultimately, they learn to develop an inner dialogue that is constructive and encouraging, rather than self-destructive and discouraging.

Transform Negative Thinking

If learners do not perceive choice, they will not take responsibility for their actions or growth. Allowing children to choose their own statements is essential to the recognition that their beliefs about control are not necessarily based in reality. However, gradually introduce the idea that the reality he/she has come to know is changeable, and that, although their prior decisions may have made sense at the time, they may not fit any longer. Teach the LH child that negative "self-talk" is the root of the problem. But take a gentle approach and recognize that baby steps will prevent your child from becoming further frustrated and overwhelmed.

PARENT TIPS FOR TRANSFORMING NEGATIVE THINKING

✓ Teach your child to observe and recognize how automatic negative thoughts can crop up in our thinking; the feeling of helplessness is triggered by these thoughts.
✓ Help your child learn to dispute these automatic negative thoughts by gathering evidence to the contrary.
✓ Teach your child to develop different explanations for "temporary setbacks." This technique, called "re-attribution," fosters a more realistic perception of the challenges encountered.
✓ Teach your child to counteract negative thinking patterns with realistic, positive, and flexible ones.

Employ the "GET" Formula

When helpless beliefs emerge, teach your child to Gather, Explore, and Take Action—The GET Formula.

G **Gather Evidence:** Help your child gather evidence that is contrary to a particular negative thought or belief. Turn it into a game where the child acts as his/her own defense attorney, putting the helpless belief on the stand.

E **Explore Options:** Once contrary evidence has been gathered, point out to your child that there are numerous plausible explanations that may or may not, in fact, cut to the core of the problem. Compare and contrast circumstances over which they have some control versus those over which they don't. Help them brainstorm ways they might meet the challenges over which they do have some control. Keep in mind that the child's explanatory style will err on the side of their habitually negative thinking.

T **Take Action:** Once your child has found alternative explanations that are based in reality, they will begin to see the illogic of their original thinking. In essence, the learner is punching holes in his or her own generalizations about helplessness and transforming that which they deemed uncontrollable into something controllable.

Be persistent. Learned helplessness does not represent a momentary state of demotivation; rather, it is a chronic and severe condition that may take months to alleviate. However, LH *is* treatable, and progress can be achieved quickly when all involved parties act together in a unified and appropriate fashion.

 # MEMORY JOGGER

Remember this face? This is "Courtney," one of the learners introduced in the pre-test at the front of the book. She's also the student who fits the profile for learned helplessness. Like the others, Courtney is unique—she exhibits a pattern of symptoms that are associated with a specific disorder. However, some of these symptoms can be observed in other conditions as well. This is why you want to look for *patterns* rather than *isolated behaviors*. To help you remember what's important in the assessment of LH, take a moment, relax, and focus on the photo, the symptoms, and the key points of this chapter.

Symptoms

◆ Displays a high level of apathy, listlessness, or lack of inertia
◆ Passive and unresponsive in spite of shocking or surprising events
◆ Does not initiate new activities or learning
◆ Increased sarcasm

◆ Does not feel in control of her environment; likely to say, "What's the point?" "Why bother?" "Who cares" or "So what?"
◆ Lack of hostility even when hostility is warranted

SUPPLEMENTAL RESOURCES

Books

Learned Helplessness: A Theory for the Age of Personal Control, by Peterson, Maier, and Seligman

Learned Optimism, by C. Peterson, S. Maier, and M. Seligman

Human Learned Helplessness, by Mario Mikulincer

Learned Helplessness and School Failure, by Robert and Myrna Gordon.

Websites

www.ldaca.org

www.supercamp.com *(A Learning Forum)*

www.outwardbound.org *(An outdoor learning and adventure camp)*

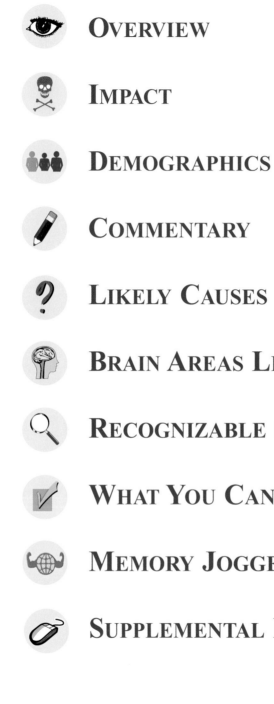

The Challenged Reader: Dyslexia

 ## OVERVIEW

Dyslexia is an imprecise term used to describe a complex and controversial learning disorder that most commonly applies to reading. The diagnosis of dyslexia is used to describe a cluster of chronic difficulties in age-appropriate reading skills despite access to instructional, linguistic, and environmental opportunities. It can include broader reading acquisition problems, such as the inability to interpret spatial relationships or to integrate visual and auditory information; however, it *doesn't* encompass *all* reading problems. Dyslexia can range from a minor disability, such as reflected in a disturbed understanding of what is read, to a complete and pervasive inability to read despite adequate intelligence. The condition is *not* outgrown and usually persists into adulthood. With intervention, however, most students effectively adapt to the impairment.

The official definition of dyslexia can be overwhelming: "A language-based disorder of constitutional origin characterized by difficulties in single word decoding, usually reflecting insufficient phonological-processing abilities. Dyslexia is manifest by variable difficulty with different forms of language, often including, in addition to reading problems, a conspicuous problem with acquiring proficiency in writing and spelling." The condition encompasses the following subtypes:

COMMON SUBTYPES OF DYSLEXIA

▼ **Deep dyslexia:** Characterized by a constellation of symptoms, including semantic errors (i.e., misreading "angry" for "mad"), an inability to pronounce nonsense words (i.e., nupeltot), and an impaired ability to comprehend abstract words in comparison to concrete words (i.e., cement vs. sidewalk).

▼ **Surface dyslexia:** Characterized by difficulty "sounding out" when reading aloud. For example, the student may be unable to sound out words with irregular pronunciations, like yacht, island, and colonel.

▼ **Alexia:** Characterized by slower letter-by-letter reading. The condition is related to the disconnection of the right hemisphere's visual-information system with the left hemisphere's word-recognition system.

▼ **Neglect dyslexia:** Characterized by a failure to explicitly identify the initial portion of a letter string. These students, for example, might substitute one word for another if the endings are the same.

▼ **Attentional dyslexia:** Characterized by deficits in short-term memory and the preservation of single-word meanings even in the context of a different sentence meaning.

The terms "reading disability" and "dyslexia" are often used interchangeably, but a subtle distinction between the two does exist. Dyslexia is characterized by impaired development of reading ability, despite an otherwise normal intellect. Conversely, reading disorders are often characterized by cognitive impairment caused by congenital, environmental, or pathological problems. For example, reading disorders may result from mental retardation, hearing problems, visual problems, environmental and/or educational deprivation, or disease. Because there is no standard test for dyslexia, the diagnosis is usually made by comparing reading ability with intelligence and standard reading expectations.

Dyslexia ranges from mild to severe. Most dyslexics display poor writing ability as well as reading difficulties, and are often, but not always, poor spellers. However, poor spelling ability alone does not indicate dyslexia. Competent readers are often below-average spellers. Some dyslexics will read notes and numbers correctly, but see printed words upside down, backwards, or distorted in some other way. They may have trouble naming letters, but not copying them.

IMPACT

Studies indicate that kindergarten children diagnosed with dyslexia achieved lower grades in school and were less likely to graduate on time. However, lack of motivation is not the problem; it simply becomes more difficult for the dyslexic student to keep up. Currently, some funding laws and district policies prohibit school intervention (pull out) programs for students before age 9 (or third grade). This can be problematic for the dyslexic reader. Another problem is that to meet the criteria for dyslexia, a gap of about 20 points between IQ and reading achievement must be shown. This definition, however, does not take into consideration that dyslexia can be present in mild forms. Many slightly dyslexic, marginal readers could benefit from early treatment, but unfortunately due to outdated assessment standards, they don't meet the criteria.

A longitudinal study revealed that about 75 percent of students labeled "dyslexic" in third grade were still dyslexic in the ninth grade. But some who were considered "normal" in third grade were later diagnosed as "dyslexic." This does not mean that dyslexia comes and goes, but that the severity may range over time. Typically the condition sticks around. Severity, however, can be environmentally-dependent—related, for example, to variables such as teaching style or stress levels. Educators ought to manage reading progress in the same way a doctor manages a patient's high blood pressure—treat the problem immediately while searching for underlying causes. The good news is that the majority of dyslexics learn to effectively compensate for their disability and go on to lead productive and successful lives.

 # DEMOGRAPHICS

With no specific diagnostic tool to identify dyslexia, and no universal definition of the condition, accurate statistics as to its prevalence are difficult. The statistics that are published are not consistent. However, they paint a picture of the general problem.

▼ **Twenty percent of 4- to 12-year-olds exhibit poor phonemic awareness.**
▼ **Approximately 5 to 12 percent of the school-aged population may be dyslexic.**
▼ **Kindergarten and first-grade readers in the bottom 20 percent of their class are likely to be reading 2.5 years behind the norm by fifth grade if untreated.**
▼ **About 26 percent of eighth-graders and 23 percent of twelfth-graders read below basic grade level, suggesting that little improvement in high school occurs.**

Some literature suggests that dyslexic boys outnumber dyslexic girls somewhere between 2-to-1 and 9-to-1. This disproportionate number of boys, however, may actually be a reflection of gender bias. Today, most researchers believe that dyslexia occurs close to equally in both sexes. In a Connecticut longitudinal study, Dr. Sally Shaywitz found a research-identified incidence of reading disability of 8.7 percent of boys and 6.9 percent of girls. However, a teacher-identified incidence of the same population identified 13.6 percent of boys and only 3.2 percent of girls. It's possible that teachers more frequently report behavioral difficulties among boys in the classroom, one symptom of dyslexia. Commonly, boys act out their frustrations and girls retreat from attention. Until a universally agreed upon definition and evaluation instrument is identified, a precise understanding of dyslexia will be difficult.

Although dyslexia and Attention-Deficit Disorder are separate conditions, approximately 40 percent of dyslexics also have ADD. It is unknown at this time what the common neurology is; however, clearly, there are some attentional and impulsivity issues related to both conditions. For more on ADD, see Chapter 1.

CONSIDER THESE FACTS REGARDING DYSLEXIA

▼ **Mirror writing is not exclusively symptomatic of dyslexia.**
▼ **Eye re-training is rarely the solution.**
▼ **Dyslexia strikes both boys and girls.**
▼ **The condition is not outgrown.**
▼ **The condition is unrelated to intelligence.**
▼ **Dyslexics are often bright, energetic, and hard working individuals.**

 ## COMMENTARY

A few interesting anomalies are associated with dyslexia. For example, left-handed people are slightly more likely than right-handed ones to have the condition. Dyslexia also appears to be less common in Japan, which may be attributable to the character form of written Japanese language. The condition is not necessarily associated with low intelligence. Many successful and famous people have dyslexia; they simply learn to compensate. Dyslexics don't necessarily dislike reading; on the contrary, many actually love to read. It's just more difficult and time consuming for them. It is encouraging that early detection and intervention increase school success rates in dyslexics.

Rarely does only one condition result in failed learning. Many dyslexics, however, experience comorbid conditions, such as depression, learned helplessness, and Attention-Deficit Disorder, which can complicate diagnosis and treatment. You can definitely help the dyslexic learner, but it would be a good idea to rally additional support.

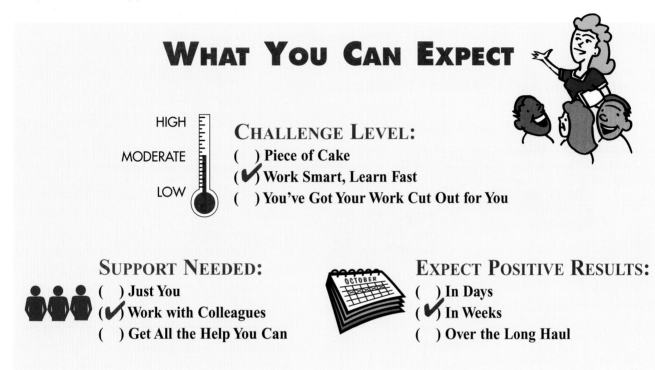

WHAT YOU CAN EXPECT

CHALLENGE LEVEL:
( ) Piece of Cake
(✓) Work Smart, Learn Fast
( ) You've Got Your Work Cut Out for You

HIGH / MODERATE / LOW

SUPPORT NEEDED:
( ) Just You
(✓) Work with Colleagues
( ) Get All the Help You Can

EXPECT POSITIVE RESULTS:
( ) In Days
(✓) In Weeks
( ) Over the Long Haul

❓ LIKELY CAUSES

Heredity

Reading disorders tend to run in families, so there is likely a genetic component. Several genetic markers have been identified as potential components of the condition, and chromosomes 1, 2, 6, and 15 have been identified as the likely carriers. Dyslexia, however, is most likely caused by a combination of external and genetic factors.

Auditory-Processing Deficits

Dyslexia is highly correlated with auditory-processing deficits. Dyslexics exhibit weak attentional capture of new auditory information, prolonged attentional dwell time, and sluggish attentional shifting—all three of which result in poor reading skills. Dyslexics also exhibit impaired functioning of the visual system, which feeds the auditory area of the posterior parietal lobes—a combination of problems also believed to contribute to the problem. For more on auditory-processing deficits, see Chapter 7.

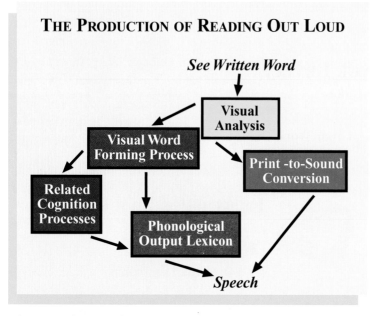

THE PRODUCTION OF READING OUT LOUD

Phonological Awareness Problems

Dyslexia is also correlated with weak phonological awareness, characterized by an inability to represent and rapidly access individual sounds in words. It is sometimes evidenced by a deficiency in one or more (but not all) of the following phenomena: sound localization and lateralization, auditory discrimination, auditory pattern recognition, recognition of temporal aspects of audition, auditory performance decrease with competing and/or degraded acoustic signals. This is the area targeted by software programs like Earobics and Fast Forword. Individuals with phonological awareness problems may hear just fine in most ranges, but certain sounds go by too fast for them to process. For example, they might not be able to hear the differences between ba, ta, and ka when verbalized at a normal rate. As a result, spelling the words properly is difficult.

Inner-Ear Dysfunction

A common thread among dyslexics is dysfunction in the cerebellar-vestibular pathway. The inner ear acts as a "fine-tuner" for all motor signals (balance/coordination/rhythm) leaving the brain and all sensory and related cognitive signals entering it. Because many dyslexics also have poor balance, sensory-motor dysfunction, spatial-temporal deficits, and coordination and rhythm deficits, their eyes struggle with the eye-movement motions of reading.

Visual System Dysfunction

While many studies have focused on phonological and inner-ear deficits, there is also support for differences in the regional functional organization of the cortical visual system. Dyslexics not only show differences on task performance with visual motion detection, but fMRI scans also show significant activation differences.

Scotopic Sensitivity

About 5 percent of dyslexics also have light or scotopic sensitivity. These individuals have a hard time seeing small black print on white paper; the print appears to shimmer or move. Some are distracted by the glaring white space. These learners tend to dis-

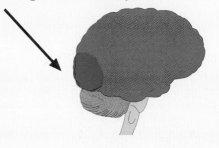

VISUAL SYSTEM DYSFUNCTION

Low level visual processing deficit in right occipital region with greater right vs. left hemisphere activity.

like florescent lighting and often "shade" the page with their hand or head when they read. Although more research is necessary to support the scotopic sensitivity argument, the Irlen Group suggests the problem is real. Other researchers support the theory that defects in the magnocellular system may be related to scotopic sensitivity, but this is yet to be proved.

Visual Memory Problems

Another theory suggests that dyslexia represents an inability to rapidly access and retrieve names for visual symbols—a significant transfer failure attributed to phonological difficulties in word sound segmentation. This means, for example, that even when subjects are taught the words "boat" and "far", they cannot reliably sound out similar sounding words, such as "moat" and "car." Some studies also indicate abnormal processing of visual motion, associated with anomalies in the magnocellular visual subsystem. This system is involved in the detection and processing of low-resolution information. And still other research suggests that dyslexia may be caused by defective nerve cells which form a pathway from the retina to the brain's visual cortex.

Brain Connectivity

Anomalous or sluggish brain connectivity between the brain's two language centers, Wernicke's area and Broca's area, might be an underling cause of dyslexia. A complex task such as reading requires precise functioning and flow of information between multiple brain sites, including the auditory areas, the visual areas, and the rest of the brain.

Prenatal Deviations

The brains of dyslexics may differentiate abnormally while still in the womb. This theory implicates deviations in neuronal pruning and neuronal migration during the second trimester of pregnancy. Some suspect that frontal lobe cells in the wrong place at the wrong time through improper cell migration are to blame.

Abnormal Neural Activity

As revealed by PET scans, the dyslexic brain is less energy efficient. An under-activity in the back half of the temporal lobe and a heavier reliance on the frontal lobe (expressive language function) have been noted, impacting both Wernicke's and Broca's areas. Also studies reveal intensified brain activity in the right hemisphere during a reading exercise, while the left hemisphere, which is normally used for reading, remains dormant. Dyslexics have been shown to use 4.6 times more brain area to do the same language task as normal controls.

 # BRAIN AREAS LIKELY INVOLVED

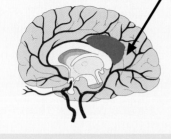

Reduced blood flow in temporal and inferior parietal regions

Temporal and Parietal Regions

Functional imaging studies of dyslexics have indicated reduced regional cerebral blood flow in the temporal and inferior parietal regions of the brain. Parietal asymmetry is also commonly found in dyslexics.

Corpus Callosum

Some studies also reveal an enlarged corpus callosum in dyslexics that is thicker and more rounded than normal. Others show over-symmetry between left and right hemispheres.

Right Occipital Cortex

Studies of dyslexics also suggest a specific low level visual processing deficit in the right occipital region.

Left Occipital Lobe

A congenital brain lesion in the left occipital lobe has been shown to cause developmental surface dyslexia which, as previously described, is characterized by difficulty "sounding out" when reading aloud.

Inner Ear/Cerebellar-Vestibular System

Inner-ear dysfunction was found to characterize 96 percent of a large dyslexic sample. This area of the brain is highly involved in sensory input-output as well as balance and coordination. Dysfunction in this area may scramble signals. Even normal thinking brains will have difficulty processing poorly scrambled or distorted signals. The resulting symptoms are dependent upon (1) the degree of signal-scrambling; (2) the location and function of the varied normal brain centers receiving and processing these scrambled signals; and (3) the brain's compensatory ability for descrambling.

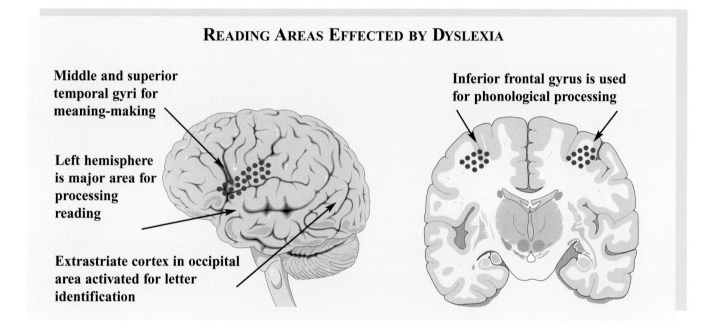

READING AREAS EFFECTED BY DYSLEXIA

Middle and superior temporal gyri for meaning-making

Left hemisphere is major area for processing reading

Extrastriate cortex in occipital area activated for letter identification

Inferior frontal gyrus is used for phonological processing

 # RECOGNIZABLE SYMPTOMS

You probably recognize by now that there are diverse and multiple phenomena associated with dyslexia and the condition can range from mild to severe. No two dyslexics exhibit exactly the same physiology. Presently, the Auditory-Analysis Test is the most sensitive evaluation instrument available to identify the condition. This test asks subjects to segment words into underlying phonological units and then delete the specific requested phonemes. Such phonological skills are presently the best predictor of reading ability.

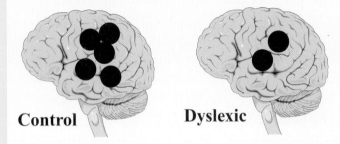

Greater number of brain areas sensitive to semantic rules found in controls vs. dyslexics.

Control   Dyslexic

At King's College in the state of Washington, researchers are exploring the effectiveness of a blink test for early identification of potential reading problems. Such a test, if proven effective, could improve the rate of early intervention, and thus, school success rates for dyslexics. If two or more warning signs are present, and there is a family history of dyslexia or ADD, a thorough assessment should be provided when the child is in first grade.

The many ways in which a person can be impaired in the processing of language suggests that there are probably a number of different ways that the brain can be organized (or disorganized as the case may be). Thus, clinicians look for a "constellation" or cluster of symptoms in the following areas:

COMMON SYMPTOMS OF DYSLEXIA

Memory
▼ Poor memory; quick learner but quick forgetter
▼ Weak in rote memorization and rapid oral retrieval
▼ Extreme difficulty memorizing non-meaningful facts
▼ Difficulty following oral directions and remembering instructions
▼ General memory instability for spelling, grammar, math, names, dates, and lists, or sequences such as the alphabet, days of the week, months of the year, and directions

Visual Processing
▼ Reversals of letters such as b and d, words such as saw and was, and numbers such as 6 and 9 or 16 and 61
▼ Letter and word blurring, doubling, scrambling, movement, omission, insertion, size change, etc.
▼ A tendency to skip over or scramble letters, words, and sentences
▼ Poor concentration, high distractibility, light sensitivity, tunnel vision, and/or delayed visual (and phonetic) processing
▼ Instability for letters, words, or numbers

Phonological Processing

▼ Slow to catch subtle differences in sounds of words
▼ Mixes up sounds in multi-syllabic words *(i.e., am-in-nall for animal, mawn lower for lawn mower, buh-sketti for spaghetti, flustrated for frustrated)*
▼ Inability to rhyme by age 4
▼ Inability to correctly complete phonemic awareness tasks

Writing

▼ Messy, poorly angulated, or drifting handwriting prone to size, spacing, and letter-sequencing errors
▼ Motor-coordination deficits are associated with a disposition to make dysphonemic spelling errors *(Impaired timing precision identifies a behavioral phenotype in some familial dyslexia subtypes)*

Reading

▼ Slow and fatiguing reading
▼ Compensatory head tilting, near-far focusing, and finger pointing
▼ Sequencing difficulties
▼ Difficulty with multiple choice questions and long-timed reading passages, as it takes more time to process the words

Cognition

▼ Spoken or written language taken literally; problems with generalization—applying information to new or different situations
▼ Difficulty learning the names and/or sounds of letters and writing the alphabet in order
▼ Inability to work with or be playful with word sounds, rhymes, and sound-alikes

Speech

▼ Slurring, stuttering, minor articulation errors, poor word recall
▼ Auditory input/motor output speech lags
▼ Delayed speech (no words spoken by the child's first birthday)
▼ Impaired timing precision in motor action *(impinges on reading and writing deficits in developmental dyslexia)*

Kinesthetic Processing

▼ Difficulty learning tasks that have a series of ordered steps, such as tying shoes
▼ Chronic difficulty with many aspects of directionality, such as confusion with left and right, over and under, before and after
▼ Poor follow through; problems prioritizing and completing tasks; wasting time
▼ Lack of dominant handedness *(switching hands between tasks or even while doing the same task)*
▼ Impaired timing precision in bimanual coordination and in motor speech

EARLY DETECTION TIPS

✓ *For 3- to 4-Year-Olds*

At this age, dyslexia signs may include trouble difficulty a book, trouble telling the difference between letters and other symbols, and not recognizing one's own name.

✓ *For Kindergartners*

At this age, dyslexia signs may include trouble distinguishing the sound parts of a word like "huh-aah-tuh" for hat and a small vocabulary.

✓ *For First and Second Graders*

At this age, dyslexia signs may include complaints that reading is easier for others, an avoidance of reading, and trouble sounding out words or an unwillingness to do so.

✓ *For Third Graders*

At this age, dyslexia signs include wild or random guesses at words, decoding problems, misunderstanding of meaning, and an avoidance of reading.

 ## WHAT YOU CAN DO

Teach literacy at all levels, not just between kindergarten and second grade. Despite mandates in many districts to provide literacy training for educators, most teachers simply don't emphasize literacy skills. The reasons for this include lack of awareness about the extent of the problem, lack of training or motivation, and lack of perceived time in response to high-stakes testing pressures.

Dyslexia is not a disease; nor will medication curb or cure it. Rather, dyslexia is the result of a different style of thinking and learning, and is best addressed through educational counseling, retraining the brain, behavior modification, and tutoring. Unfortunately, no one strategy works for everyone and experience tells us that treating dyslexia with a "cookie-cutter" approach is ineffective. Nevertheless, many educators report good success with a balanced reading program that combines both holistic/meaning and analytic/phonetic approaches with other activities to improve language development. Other helpful strategies include the following:

AS AN EDUCATOR

Start early and be persistent. Remedial action in response to reading difficulties should involve intensive individualized tutoring as early as possible. Phonemic awareness games and programs are especially important at the pre-K through third-grade levels. "Dr. Seuss" books, which feature great rhyming schemes, are great for enhancing phonemic awareness in the early grades. Some schools have experienced a jump in reading scores that may be related to an increase in rhyming and song games. Fun language games like "pig Latin" (pronounced ig-pay, atin-lay!) may help students develop greater sound awareness, which ultimately impacts reading.

TEACHING TIPS FOR POSITIVE EARLY READING EXPERIENCES

Necessary Methodology:
✓ Individualized instruction
✓ Intensive phonic instruction combined with high-interest reading matter
✓ Positive expectations
✓ Long-term approach with frequent follow-up assessments

Helpful Methodology:
✓ Linguistic and meaning-based approaches
✓ Systemic and sequential approaches
✓ Cumulative and process-oriented methods
✓ Balanced reading programs
✓ Multi-sensory techniques

Appropriate at the Pre-K Level

✓ Read all books aloud.
✓ Rhyming material is good.
✓ Teach songs with simple words.
✓ Write down children's spoken words.
✓ Avoid "drudgery" assignments *(i.e., workbooks)*.

Appropriate In Kindergarten

✓ Continue to read aloud.
✓ Emphasize songs, noting especially the words.
✓ Continue to read rhyming material.
✓ Evaluate hearing and vision.
✓ Read enjoyable material *(books that are meaningful and fun for learners)*.
✓ Keep your eyes and ears open for problems.

Appropriate In First and Second Grades

✓ Read, read, and read more.
✓ Provide phonemic awareness testing for all students.
✓ Balance phonics-based approaches with whole-language reading programs.
✓ Keep your eyes and ears open for problems.

Appropriate In Third Grade

✓ Continue reading.
✓ Request testing if a child exhibits a dislike of reading.
✓ Keep your eyes and ears open for problems.

Appropriate at the Secondary Level

✓ Teach a three-tier reading process that includes scanning, organizing, and discussion *(Pre-reading and scanning helps students grasp necessary background information)*.
✓ Provide a list of reading questions to help learners focus and increase comprehension.

✓ Have learners read small chunks of material and create their own questions or reword yours.

✓ Ask some "what if" questions to encourage deeper analysis and critical thinking skills.

✓ Encourage learners to do post-reading, review, and discussion of the reading matter.

Even at the secondary level it is appropriate to assume that your students are not good readers. One study indicates, in fact, that a mere 6 percent of high-school seniors read at an advanced level. Most are marginal or average. One successful program at Thurgood Marshall High School in San Francisco mandated all incoming ninth graders to participate in a class meeting three times a week where reading logs were maintained. If problems surfaced, based on the student's own analysis, follow-up was provided. Students in the program made four years of gains in two years and more students reported that they liked reading and read more as a result. The message is clear: Don't assume kids can read or are good readers, even at the high-school level.

Consider Phonological-Awareness Training

Phonological awareness, a key factor in some reading problems, is addressed by a number of commercial training programs including Earobics, Fast Forword, and the Lindamood Phoneme Sequencing (LiPS) Program. Such programs ask readers to identify the feel of the sounds they read. For example, "P is a lip popper." This approach aims to help learners more clearly distinguish the phonemes of words. Its effectiveness is probably related to its ability to get to the core of the problem—specific word distinctions and sounds needed for linking up see-hear with comprehension. Reading programs in general should address phonological awareness; however dyslexics need more of it more often. None of these programs are cheap and all require staff support. Customized programs are also prevalent and are often used by school speech and hearing therapists.

As a Parent

Be a strong advocate for your child so that they receive all the help they need. Understand and treat dyslexia for what it is—a cluster of learning challenges that should be dealt with early and rigorously. Don't panic, but don't ignore the problem either. Treat your child as if they have an illness. Early intervention is absolutely KEY!!! The condition, of course, is not life-threatening, but school success may be jeopardized if it is not addressed early on. As always, let your child know

they're loved and valued despite what they do or don't do. Does this mean we ought to overlook inappropriate behaviors? Of course not! Discipline, however, does not have to mean punishment. Use positive reinforcement and remember your child is facing a substantial challenge.

Rely on School Intervention Programs

Schools usually have a number of professionals on board (i.e., reading specialists, speech pathologists, or school psychologists) that are trained to work with dyslexic learners. If you suspect a problem, request testing. Follow up to see what the testing indicates. If it appears to be positive, request that a plan be put in place to assist your child. Be careful not to undermine the help of school personnel. As frustrating as the system can sometimes be, specialized school personnel are important to your child's treatment.

Develop Your Own Response Plan

Read as much as you can about your child's condition. Talk to other parents of children with dyslexia and treatment specialists in the field. Do research on the Internet or in the library. Once you have a thorough understanding of the condition and the various interventions, develop your own response plan. Intense phonics instruction with high-interest reading material over the long-term is paramount.

Consider Many Options

Some find that a combination of anti-motion sickness medications and retraining in balance, spinning, and rhythm movements help the dyslexic learner. The goal is to retrain the inner ear or vestibular system for motion-sensing skills and input-output information processing.

Obtain Regular Eye Examinations

Although the current model for dyslexia treatment is primarily phonological, rather than visual, do have your child's vision tested regularly. Some optometrists recommend visual training for reading problems; however, there is not strong research to support the success of visual training as an intervention for dyslexia. Nevertheless, it is important to rule out poor eyesight as a potential factor or, if necessary, to correct your child's vision with glasses.

The Value of Colored Contact Lenses

In one study dyslexic subjects were given a reading test under three different conditions: (1) While fitted with colored contact lenses; (2) Without contact lenses; and (3) While fitted with lightly tinted "placebo" contact lenses that subjects were told had been specially designed to help with reading. The placebo increased reading speed by 6 words per minute, while the colored contact lenses improved reading speed by 12 words per minute, representing a 15 percent improvement overall. As reflected by this and many other studies employing placebo controls, a student's belief in the treatment is essential to their success.

Experiment with the One-Eye Reading Approach

Some dyslexics have found that patching one eye can improve their eye control during reading. One study gave special glasses to 144 severely dyslexic children with unstable eye control. Half of the subjects received lenses with the left side covered by opaque tape, while the other half got clear lenses on both sides. At the end of the nine-month study, those with the eye patch were eight months ahead of the control group in reading ability.

Seek Medical Advice

Sometimes dyslexics experience symptoms such as headache or nausea during reading, in which case a prescription or over-the-counter medication may be helpful. Medications do not treat dyslexia, however. They merely relieve some symptoms. Unfortunately, some people mistake the alleviating of symptoms for a cure and, therefore, wrongly promote the value of medicinal remedies. This can be a problem if it prevents students from seeking or obtaining the educational support they need.

MEMORY JOGGER

Remember this face? This is "Lee," one of the learners introduced in the pre-test at the front of the book. He's also the student who fits the profile for dyslexia. Like the others, Lee is unique—he exhibits a pattern of symptoms that are associated with a specific disorder. However, some of these symptoms can be observed in other conditions as well. This is why you want to look for *patterns* rather than *isolated behaviors*. To help you remember what's important in the assessment of dyslexia, take a moment, relax, and focus on the photo, the symptoms, and the key points of this chapter.

Symptoms

◆ Trouble with sequencing, prioritizing, and completing tasks

◆ Takes spoken or written language literally

◆ Difficulty following oral directions and remembering them

◆ Inability to rhyme by age four

◆ Lack of dominant handedness; switches hands between or even during tasks

◆ Confuses left and right, over and under, before and after, and other directionality words and concepts

◆ Unable to correctly complete phonemic-awareness tasks

◆ Difficulty learning the names and sounds of letters and writing them in alphabetical order

SUPPLEMENTAL RESOURCES

Books/Journals

Reversals: A Personal Account of Victory Over Dyslexia, by Eileen M. Simpson
Learning to Read, by Laurence Rieben, ed.
Dyslexia: Practical and Easy-to-Follow Advice, by Robin Temple
Smart But Feeling Dumb, by Harold Levinson
The Discovery of Cerebellar-Vestibular Syndromes and Therapies, by Harold Levinson
Turning Around Upside-Down Kids, by Harold Levinson
To Read or Not to Read, by Daphne M. Hurford
Beyond Dyslexia, by Dorothy Van Den Honert
To Read or Not to Read, by Daphne Hurford
Annals of Dyslexia
*Journal of Learning Disabilitie*s

Researchers

Gordon Sherman, former President of International Dyslexia Association, now Executive Director of the Outreach Program at the Newgrange School

John Stein, University Laboratory of Physiology, Oxford; and Department of Orthoptics, Royal Berkshire Hospital, Reading, UK

Dr. Sally Shaywitz, Yale University

Websites

www.pie.org   www.dys-add.com   www.fastforword.com
www.smbs.buffalo.edu   www.dyslexia.com

Organizations

The Dyslexia Institute (www.dyslexia-inst.org)
    Davis Dyslexia Association International (www.dyslexia.com)
        International Dyslexia Association (www.interdys.org) • 410-296-0232
            Learning Disabilities Association (www.ldanatl.org) • 888-300-6710
            National Center for Learning Disabilities (www.ncld.org) • 888-575-7373

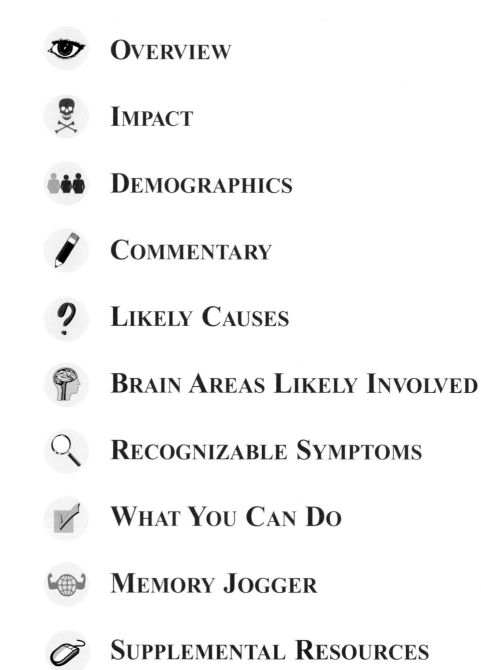

4

The Argumentative Learner: Oppositional Disorder

OVERVIEW

Oppositional Disorder (OPD) is a serious and chronic psychiatric condition that is characterized by verbal aggressiveness, a tendency to bother others, a confrontational attitude, and a disregard for how others feel. Individuals with OPD are victims; they don't choose to act out in this manner. Evidence suggests that the condition is a result of a combination of environment and genetics. A negative, traumatic, or neglectful environment can be a major contributing factor, but is not always the case.

IMPACT

This disorder can be extremely trying for anyone who comes into contact with the OPD sufferer. Sufferers do not respond to reasonable persuasion, regardless of self-interest; and their opposition to all authority figures, especially parents and teachers, is pervasive and constant. Academic failure and poor social adjustment are common complications. Some improvement is possible when intervention occurs early. The more time that passes without treatment, however, the more entrenched and acute the disorder becomes. Physicians report that it is rare to see a patient with only OPD. Usually the disorder is accompanied by other neuropsychiatric conditions as well. Approximately 30 to 40 percent of children with OPD are also diagnosed with Attention-Deficit Disorder (ADD). And about 15 to 20 percent of children with OPD are also diagnosed with a mood (affective) disorder or anxiety disorder.

 # DEMOGRAPHICS

Over the past 25 years or so, a steady increase in symptoms of oppositional and defiant behaviors in school-aged populations has occurred. Reliable numbers are difficult to obtain; however, it is estimated that approximately two to four million Americans are afflicted with OPD. In fact, OPD/ADD is the most common combined psychiatric problem in children. About 40 to 50 percent of ADD sufferers also develop OPD. How pervasive is the problem? It appears that between 8 and 15 percent of all children have either or both conditions. It is more common in boys than in girls at the younger ages, but then balances out across genders in adolescence.

Typical defiance or resistance should not be confused with OPD. For example, oppositional behaviors exhibited in 18- to 36-month-old children are part of a normal developmental phase. It is the persistence of severe and pervasive oppositional behaviors that signifies a problem. Onset appears as early as age 3, but more commonly begins in late childhood or early adolescence. In some children, OPD evolves into Conduct Disorder or a mood (affective) disorder.

OPD appears to run in families and is three times more likely to afflict children who have an alcoholic parent and/or a parent who has been in trouble with the law. The reason for this correlation may be that the troubled parent had OPD as a child and is now suffering from Antisocial Personality Disorder. In other words, the correlation may be more genetic than environmental. Some indications are that OPD can develop into an anxiety disorder or Antisocial Personality Disorder in adulthood. There is also a correlation, although not causal, with Obsessive-Compulsive Disorder. In many cases, however, reasonable social and occupational adjustment can be made with appropriate intervention and treatment.

 # COMMENTARY

OPD is characterized by the sufferer's annoyance of others (perceived to be *intentional*) and by aggressiveness, rather than by impulsiveness. ADD sufferers, by comparison, don't necessarily *intend* to annoy others—their behavior is rather a by-product of their impulsiveness. OPD sufferers, on the other hand, seem to get pleasure from their behavior. An ADD sufferer may, for example, impulsively push a child too hard on a swing knocking them to the ground, but he/she would then feel sorry that the accident occurred. An OPD sufferer, on the other hand, would likely deny he/she did it and then brag about it later to friends.

While ADD symptoms include chronic restlessness and poor social skills, OPD sufferers don't necessarily have these problems. However, OPD is more difficult to live with in both the classroom and home environment. Clearly, those diagnosed with both conditions represent a huge challenge. The combined effect of impulsivity, hyperactivity, oppositional behavior, and defiance often leads to fights, rough play, and serious temper tantrums. While some ADD sufferers appear to recover in most part from the condition, OPD sufferers rarely do.

OPD constitutes a moderate to high level of challenge to the classroom teacher. You can contribute to this learner's success, but you will need support from others—notably the parents and mental-health professionals.

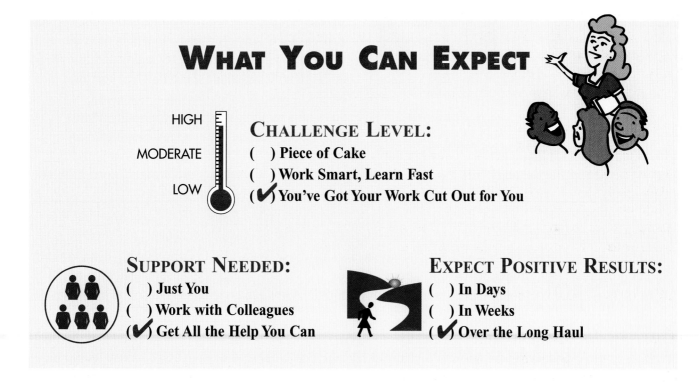

WHAT YOU CAN EXPECT

HIGH
MODERATE
LOW

CHALLENGE LEVEL:
( ) Piece of Cake
( ) Work Smart, Learn Fast
(✔) You've Got Your Work Cut Out for You

SUPPORT NEEDED:
( ) Just You
( ) Work with Colleagues
(✔) Get All the Help You Can

EXPECT POSITIVE RESULTS:
( ) In Days
( ) In Weeks
(✔) Over the Long Haul

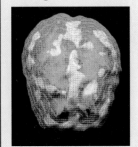

BRAIN ACTIVITY IN OPPOSITIONAL DISORDER

Top-down view of teenage brain. Note increased activity (in red) throughout edges and middle.

Underside view of same teenager's brain. Note increased activity (in red) in basal ganglia.

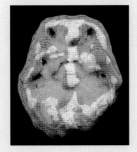

Source: *Images into Human Behavior: A Brain SPECT Atlas,* Daniel G. Amen, MD, 2000

? LIKELY CAUSES

The specific cause of OPD is unknown at this time. The following theories, however, have been proposed:

Temperament

Most experts think that inherent personality or temperament contributes to the disorder, and the effects may be heightened when parents aren't educated about the condition and don't seek professional help. Since OPD often coexists with other problems, such as ADD and mood disorders, it is difficult to isolate the definitive causes.

In many cases a problem is evident almost from birth and becomes even more pronounced over time. One mom said that even as a baby her son's temperament was difficult. "When he was mad, watch out. We used to affectionately call him our 'Angry Little Man.'" These kids are simply more rigid and demanding. They have a heightened need to be in control right from the start.

Trauma Incidence

There is a higher incidence of childhood trauma among those with OPD. Exposure to head trauma, neglect, divorce, environmental toxins, sexual and/or physical abuse may predispose one to OPD. Conversely, it should be noted that a traumatic childhood does not necessarily lead to social misbehavior.

Parental Alcoholism

There is some evidence that a correlation may exist between OPD and one or both parents being alcoholic.

Chemical Dysregulation

One cause (or symptom) may be a dysfunctional serotonin system. Typically, in OPD patients, the cingulate gyrus (in the back of the frontal lobes) is hyperactive, with abnormally low levels of serotonin.

Heredity

Researchers have been studying gene variants associated with the dopamine system and their potential relationship to disorders and behaviors comorbid (overlapping) with drug abuse. A genetic basis for a "reward-deficiency syndrome" consisting of addictive, impulsive, and compulsive behavior and personality disorders is being proposed.

Neurological Disorders

Associations have been made with OPD symptoms and some neurological disorders, such as epilepsy.

 # BRAIN AREAS LIKELY INVOLVED

The brain areas involved include the cingulate gyrus, the fear-arousal system, and the basal ganglia. Increased activity in the left temporal lobe is also implicated in OPD and may contribute to irritability.

The Cingulate Gyrus

The cingulate gyrus, which runs longitudinally through the middle of the frontal lobes, serves as a "gear shifter" in the brain and allows us to move smoothly from one state to another. In OPD patients, however, the cingulate gyrus is typically overactive. This overdose of activity may intensify oppositional behaviors and make it biologically difficult for the sufferer to stop a thought at will and move on. There are medications and behavioral therapy approaches that have shown promise in reducing the overactivity of this area.

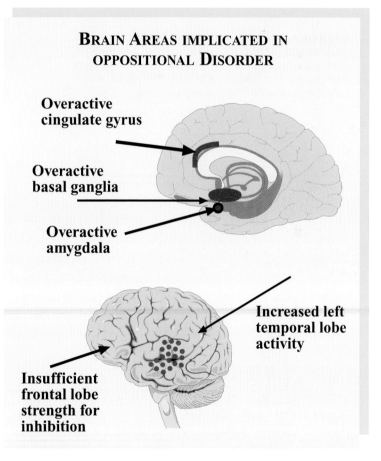

BRAIN AREAS IMPLICATED IN OPPOSITIONAL DISORDER

Overactive cingulate gyrus

Overactive basal ganglia

Overactive amygdala

Increased left temporal lobe activity

Insufficient frontal lobe strength for inhibition

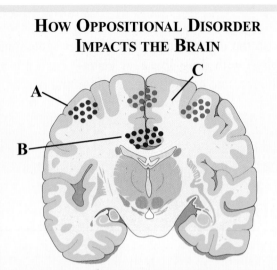

HOW OPPOSITIONAL DISORDER IMPACTS THE BRAIN

In students with OPD, reduced activity occurs in (A) the prefrontal cortex, which is thoughtful and inhibitory; (B) the basil ganglia, which helps integrate feelings and movements; and (C) the cingulate gyrus, which acts as a "gearshifter" for emotional states.

The Amygdala

Since OPD sufferers often have little, if any, fear of consequences, the amygdala (a small structure in the temporal lobes that regulates fear) has also been implicated. Excess fearlessness has been correlated with limit-breaking and boundary-breaking behaviors later in life; whereas, cautious, fearful behaviors are associated with a stronger conscience and cooperation.

The Basal Ganglia

Though the relationship at this point is still tentative, there is some evidence that the basal ganglia, located in the lower midbrain area, may be linked to the thinking and acting out of oppositional and impulsive thoughts. The basal ganglia is also highly involved with making smooth transitions in thinking, moving, and managing anxiety.

Neurotransmitter Levels

Noradrenaline (also known as norepinephrine) is the neurotransmitter of arousal, high energy, and urgency. It is produced by the adrenal glands and helps maintain constant blood pressure. It also regulates our arousal moods and emotions. The brain area that releases norepinephrine is the locus ceruleus in the midbrain. From there it is distributed throughout the brain and influences us tremendously, especially during the flight or fight response. While the baseline level of noradrenaline is typically just high enough to keep us motivated and to provide a reserve of energy, some individuals (including OPD sufferers) may produce an unusually high level of noradrenaline. Under these circumstances, even a small stimulus will create unusually strong arousal. The individual may respond to little things with anxiety, fear, or over-reactivity. Conversely, when an individual has an abnormally low level of noradrenaline, higher levels of stimulation are required to activate normal feelings of energy and aliveness.

Anatomical Anomalies

Anatomical anomalies are not prevalent or consistent in OPD patients, so a MRI is of little value. In some cases, such as when an individual is involved in a serious accident, a PET (positron emission tomography) scan or SPECT (single positron emission computerized tomography) image, may help in identifying metabolic changes. However, there is no evidence that scanning by itself can make an OPD diagnosis.

RECOGNIZABLE SYMPTOMS

OPD involves a pattern of defiant, angry, antagonistic, hostile, irritable, and/or vindictive behaviors; however, it does not necessarily include violent offenses. Sufferers typically blame others for their problems. They can be frustrating, tricky, aggressive, and deceitful, but they are not generally dangerous. While most children will comply with an adult's reasonable requests about seven out of ten times, OPD children will generally comply three or fewer times—and sometimes never. The simple questions to ask yourself are how often does the student comply with my requests? And, does the behavior occur more frequently than is typically observed in individuals of comparable age and developmental level? Consider the following diagnostic criteria, along with frequency of behaviors and duration period:

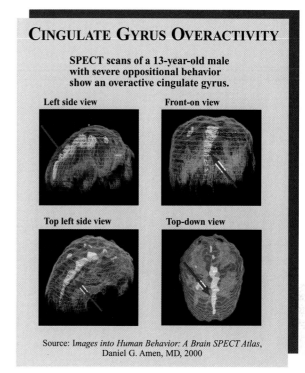

CINGULATE GYRUS OVERACTIVITY

SPECT scans of a 13-year-old male with severe oppositional behavior show an overactive cingulate gyrus.

Left side view

Front-on view

Top left side view

Top-down view

Source: *Images into Human Behavior: A Brain SPECT Atlas*, Daniel G. Amen, MD, 2000

DIAGNOSTIC CRITERIA FOR OPD

A pattern of negative, hostile, and defiant behavior lasting at least six months, during which four (or more) of the following are present:

▼ Losing one's temper
▼ Arguing with adults
▼ Defying adults or refusing adult requests or rules
▼ Deliberately annoying others
▼ Blaming others for one's own mistakes or misbehavior

▼ Being touchy or easily annoyed
▼ Being angry and resentful
▼ Being spiteful or vindictive for no apparent reason
▼ Swearing or using obscene language
▼ Holding a low opinion of oneself

What You Can Do

Although dealing with OPD is challenging for everyone involved, you can contribute to the success of this learner. OPD is not acute, so there's no need to go into emergency mode. By taking a calm and steady approach to the problem, you will help reduce the OPD sufferer's stress, as well as your own. The strategies described in the following sections can help turn what might at first feel like a hopeless situation into a constructive accommodation:

As an Educator

Seek Support/Create a Response Team

You will need the support of others, notably school administrators, other teachers, the child's parents, a medical doctor, and mental-health professionals. Once you've identified the key support team, get them together to talk face-to-face outside of the student's presence. Consistent communication between the child's parents, between school and home, and between medical/treatment professionals and other concerned parties is crucial. This team approach can help offset the OPD child's tendency to play one person or group off another. All of the child's caregivers (grandparents, relatives, baby-sitters, etc.) need to understand OPD and the treatment plan as well.

Develop a Plan

With the help of a therapist and physician, develop an intervention plan. Also discuss strategies for dealing with the oppositional and defiant behavior. If you react on the spur of the moment, your emotions will guide you wrongly in dealing with these children. They try to provoke intense feelings in everyone. A written and agreed upon plan should outline exactly what response is appropriate for each pattern of behavior. For example, what should be done if the child disrupts class, annoys others, gets in a fight, throws a major temper tantrum, makes suicidal threats, or declares he/she is going to run away? Whatever the response, the plan must be adhered to by all parties involved with the child to work. See that all parties are "on board" and agree to *not* "buy into" the oppositional behavior style exhibited by the child.

Use a Behavior-Modification Approach

A behavior-modification approach can help manage the OPD child both at home and at school. However, rewards and punishments should be mutually agreed upon and considered in light of the individual's specific temperament and personal issues. In other words, a formula approach does not work with OPD children. The rewards should not be money or material things, but rather privileges or activities that you know the child enjoys. Use a mix of negative and positive reinforcers. A typical positive reinforcer, for example, might be a later bedtime on the weekend or the opportunity to choose the dinner menu for the evening. A typical negative reinforcer would be revoking TV privileges.

Respond in a Non-Oppositional Way

Inflexible teachers or caretakers who react with intense emotions will fail in dealing effectively with the behavior of the OPD child. If a student stomps his feet and says, "You can't make me!" it's better to agree with him and instead use reverse psychology. Try, "You're right, I can't make you. Nobody can, not even you. Yeah, that's right, I don't even think you can make yourself do it!" Over and over teachers will be challenged, and over and over they must learn to take a deep breath, relax, and avoid confrontation. Seek common ground, and if it's not there, create it. If the student stomps out of the room, for example, call a break and then initiate a quick state-change activity, such as outdoor story time, a group skip around the playground, or a New Games activity. This strategy won't work every time, but try to understand that when adults respond with an oppositional approach, the problem worsens and can easily turn into a full-scale "war."

Confirm Stories

Usually the OPD individual does not regard him/herself as the problem, but rather blames others. Some try to convince other adults that their parents have mistreated them; others convince parents that their teachers are treating them unfairly. Obviously this can keep everyone off balance and delay or prevent proper intervention.

Be Consistent

Do not bend the rules with the OPD child. It is very important to remain consistent both individually and across caretaker lines. For example, if Max is not allowed to eat candy at home, grandparents, baby-sitters, and teachers need to follow this rule as well. A firm, authoritative style does not have to be in conflict with a loving, affectionate approach. The key is to be consistent in your expectations and to voice them in a kind and loving way. Consequences for breaking the rules should be fairly and dispassionately administered. Share the treatment/behavior modification plan with all involved parties, so that discipline responses remain consistent between caregivers as well.

Isolate and Prioritize Behavior Issues

Prioritize the behaviors you wish to address first; then focus your responses on the targeted behaviors. Rather than trying to teach the child to "be good," you might try, for example, to encourage the child not to hit or swear.

Be Specific with Your Requests

When you give the OPD child a request, you must be very clear and specific. For example, rather than saying, "listen when I tell you something," a better request would be, "Please sit down and look at me when I ask you to listen." If the OPD sufferer can read, create a list of simple, straightforward ground rules (or expectations) that you can make into a poster for the home and/or classroom. Consider the appropriateness of asking the individual to sign a "contract" of agreement with the ground rules.

CLASSROOM "DO'S" AND "DON'TS"

✓ **Do** provide encouragement, just as you would with any other student. **Don't** get caught up in arguing with the OPD sufferer—you'll always lose. Even if you win, you lose when the relationship suffers.

✓ **Do** use a lot of writing, journaling, and drawing. These activities are great for encouraging positive and appropriate expression. They also help the OPD sufferer sort out their thoughts and feelings. Focus on the process, rather than the product. **Don't** be adamant in your approach or expectations.

✓ **Do** let go of tight control; try to be flexible. **Don't** give ultimatums. **Do** give choices: "Would you rather do it this way or another way?" **Do** use double binds where both ways will work: "Would you rather finish this today or later this week?" Finally, avoid becoming obsessed by this student. Work instead for slow and steady progress.

✓ **Do** try to remember that an unhealthy brain causes kids (and adults) to act in unproductive ways (like resisting everything). Although this behavior can be very frustrating, **do** let the OPD child know he/she is loved and valued in spite of his/her condition. **Don't**, however, overlook their inappropriate behaviors. Also, **don't** add fuel to the fire or lock into a tug-of-war with the OPD sufferer.

AS A PARENT

Consider Psychotherapy

Treatment for OPD usually includes a combination of behavioral and drug therapies. Early diagnosis is key. However, if the patient has multiple disorders, it is usually recommended that the related problem (i.e., ADD, Tourette's Syndrome, a mood or anxiety disorder) be treated first. The effectiveness of psychotherapy for this disorder has not yet been determined; however, we do know that the dropout rate for individuals in psychotherapy for OPD is 30 percent a year.

Consider Drug Therapy

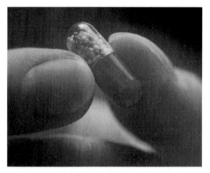

The effectiveness of drug therapies in OPD is also not known at this time. There are drugs, however, that have been proven safe in children, have no long-term side effects, and have been found in studies to be effective in extremely aggressive children/adolescents. Because OPD is partially mediated by serotonin, treatment with Serotonin Selective Reuptake Inhibitors (i.e., Zoloft, Paxil, Anafranil, Serzone, Luvox, and Prozac) is often effective and may dramatically reduce the OPD behaviors. In some cases, the treatment has normalized the patient's behaviors almost completely. Antidepressants, however, do have short-term side effects, so learn about these too. Often, the first medication tried is not the best one, so expect some trial-and-err testing in the process. In general, medications that help increase serotonin levels in the brain are most helpful. Blood pressure medications (i.e., Catapres, Tenex, and Inderal) are sometimes effective in the treatment of very aggressive children and adolescents who rarely sleep. Dixarit, a sweet-tasting version of the medication for children, has been shown to be safe even for preschool-age children; however, there is a 10 percent chance of a depressive side effect. Anti-convulsants (i.e., Tegretol and Risperidone), usually used for seizures and Bipolar Disorder, are presently being examined for their potential effect in OPD.

Consider Natural Supplements

Many parents prefer trying natural serotonin enhancers (i.e., St. John's Wort) before turning to prescription medication. The natural supplements, however, are highly dosage dependent and variable, so treatment is often more difficult to measure when using these remedies. In all matters of supplementation, consult your doctor first. A qualified nutritionist may offer valuable advice, as well.

Closely Monitor Treatments

When working with medical professionals to create an effective therapeutic drug plan, the following three basic principles ought to be applied: (1) Start low; (2) Go slow; and (3) Monitor carefully. With children, this guideline becomes especially important. Physicians will often start children out on psychotherapeutic drugs at about 25 percent of the usual recommended adult dosage. The goal is to determine the lowest effective dose. Many children respond to drugs at very low doses, and it is easier to monitor physical and psychological changes with this approach.

Encourage Exercise

Exercise can help increase serotonin levels in the brain and provides a natural way to alter the OPD sufferer's mood. Normally, the smaller amino acids (i.e., tryptophan) have to compete with the larger amino acids to enter the brain's blood barrier, but during exercise, the larger amino acids become depleted, allowing the smaller ones more access, thereby raising serotonin levels.

Make Appropriate Dietary Changes

High-carbohydrate foods increase the production of serotonin, the neurotransmitter associated with depression and anxiety. Foods that are high in carbohydrates include pasta, potatoes, whole grain breads, popcorn, rice, and pretzels. Other foods that increase serotonin because they're rich in tryptophan include peanut butter, meats, chicken, salmon, and beef. Some nutritionists recommend tryptophan supplements (1,000 mg. taken at bedtime) along with a high-quality daily multi-vitamin/mineral supplement (with high B vitamins). Another recommended supplement for OPD sufferers is 5-HTP (100 mg. per day).

Monitor Personal Stress

Parents, teachers, and caretakers will need to maintain a healthy personal stress level in order to deal effectively with the OPD child. Monitor your own stress carefully and build in personal outlets (i.e., massage, meditation, exercise, time for yourself). Try as well to create alternatives for high-stress moments/days.

5

The Frustrated Learner:
Learning Delayed

 ## OVERVIEW

Learning delayed (LD) or delayed development is a term used to describe a child's failure to make the usual developmental milestones typical of his or her age. Sometimes the term is used euphemistically for borderline to mild mental retardation. However, because of the enormous plasticity of the early human brain, many children who are "delayed" catch up later. Of course, many don't catch up, and while some functions (i.e., thinking, motor skills, emotional development) may be preserved, other areas may be impaired.

A number of potential factors contribute to delayed development and learning delays, including genetic problems, brain injuries, malnutrition, fetal alcohol exposure, autism, impoverished environments, neglect, and inadequate care. Brain injuries or brain insults, as they are generically called, are commonly caused by one or more of the following factors:

▼ **Blows to the head** *(often from domestic abuse)*
▼ **Environmental exposure** *(metals, chemicals, air pollution)*
▼ **Rapid acceleration or deceleration** *(car accidents are the most common)*
▼ **Accidents on children's recreational vehicles** *(bicycle, skateboard, sled, skates, etc.)*
▼ **Prenatal exposure to drugs and toxins** *(tobacco, narcotics, alcohol, chronic distress, etc.)*
▼ **Concussive-prone sports** *(football, soccer, baseball, hockey, etc.)*
▼ **Falls or unprotected impact** *(down stairs, bunk bed fall, hit by door, kicked by horse, etc.)*
▼ **Difficult births and maternal infection**

In spite of continued affluence in developed countries, contributing factors such as poverty, broken families, violence, and inadequate parenting skills are still prevalent. These conditions, combined with the role of genetics, contribute to the problem that affects millions of children in our schools. In short, there is a significant potential for the developing fetus and developing child to be impacted by unhealthy conditions. Considering the magnitude of this problem, having even a single healthy student in the classroom could be considered miraculous. Such students typically have been nurtured in a nuclear family, have had no exposure to toxins, and have developed strong emotional and social skills. This student, however, is unfortunately not the norm.

 # IMPACT

The impact of delayed learning on schools is growing. Presently the trend in schools is to embrace all learners, even those with significant developmental challenges, in mainstream classrooms. The problem is that most teachers are not trained to deal with the challenged student, a factor that adds to the problems of the already stressed-out staff. Consider these significant impacts: (1) Many challenged students fall through the cracks, minimal learning occurs, if any, and then they are passed on to the next grade level where the injustice is repeated; (2) Teachers grow increasingly frustrated and overwhelmed, resulting in widespread hopelessness and resignation; and (3) The number of dysfunctional citizens with a second-rate education is growing because the system that was built for yesterday's students is incapable of dealing with today's reality.

 # DEMOGRAPHICS

The statistics regarding the causes of delayed development are sobering. Remember, as with other disorders, there is a tremendous amount of comorbidity or overlap with other problems. For example, delayed development/LD is often present in families in which there is domestic abuse, maternal smoking, and/or alcohol abuse. Let's take a closer look at some of the factors.

Fetal Alcohol Syndrome

Studies suggest that Fetal Alcohol Syndrome (FAS) is presently the single most prevalent cause of mental retardation and developmental/learning delays in the United States. And, unfortunately, FAS has long-term consequences for both the individual and society. A predictable, long-term progression of the disorder into adulthood challenges communities as they struggle to respond to the maladaptive behaviors of the adult FAS victim. This serious condition is, in fact, one of the leading causes of birth defects.

Down's Syndrome and Spina Bifida are the other two. It is not known precisely how many infants are born with FAS; however, even conservative statistics estimate that the number is at least 1 in every 100 live births. And, The National Clearinghouse for Alcohol Information states that for every infant born with FAS, as many as ten others may be born with partial effects or Fetal Alcohol Effects (FAE). Many healthcare professionals feel that fetal alcohol exposure is the most serious childhood problem we're facing today.

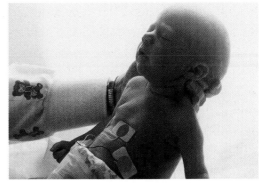

FAS babies are typically characterized by a smaller head, smaller brain, and some mental retardation or learning delay. Although the research on FAS indicates that even light drinking in pregnancy (especially during the most critical times of fetal development) can lead to FAS effects, binge drinking while pregnant is almost certain to impact the baby's health. A sudden surge of alcohol, even during a single evening celebration, can have devastating effects. It appears that timing is a factor. The months (not days!) before conception and the subsequent eight weeks following conception (when a mother is least likely to know she's pregnant) appear to be the most critical periods. It is difficult to estimate the quantity of alcohol that poses a risk since there is such a wide variance among women in their ability to metabolize alcohol. For this reason, most healthcare professionals recommend that pregnant women abstain completely during pregnancy.

In spite of these findings and the health warnings on all alcoholic beverage containers, data suggests that consumption of alcoholic beverages may be increasing among pregnant women. In 1995, according to data from yearly surveys of more than 138,000 women, 15.3 percent of pregnant women reported occasional consumption of alcohol, compared with 10 percent in 1992. The study also found that college-educated, employed, unmarried women with a household income of more than $50,000, who were also smokers, were the most likely group of women to drink during pregnancy.

One study cited that while 90 percent of women knew that drinking during pregnancy was dangerous to the fetus, 75 percent of these individuals thought only three drinks a day was safe! Even minimal consumption (as little as one ounce a day) increases the risk for abnormalities by 10 percent. Binge drinking (even one episode) poses more profound risk, and drinking during the last trimester can destroy large groups of neurons. Typically, women who consume alcohol during pregnancy also exhibit other risk factors, such as a lack of prenatal care, exposure to domestic abuse, drug use, etc. One study stated that 10 to 15 percent of FAS moms admitted they also used cocaine.

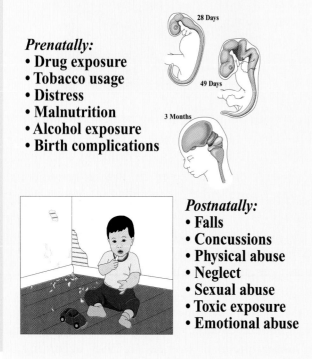

FACTORS WHICH CONTRIBUTE TO DELAYED DEVELOPMENT

28 Days

49 Days

3 Months

Prenatally:
• Drug exposure
• Tobacco usage
• Distress
• Malnutrition
• Alcohol exposure
• Birth complications

Postnatally:
• Falls
• Concussions
• Physical abuse
• Neglect
• Sexual abuse
• Toxic exposure
• Emotional abuse

Abuse and Neglect

It is estimated that about one in five students with learning disabilities acquired them as a result of severe abuse or neglect. When we look at the population of learning-disabled students as a whole, more than twice as many have been abused when compared to normal student populations. Failure of parents or guardians to take care of children's physical, educational, medical, or emotional needs is on the rise. In fact, between 1986 and 1993, the number of children seriously injured due to abuse quadrupled. And, in 1999, 1.6 million new cases of childhood maltreatment were reported in the United States alone. Girls were more likely to be victims of sexual abuse, whereas boys were more likely to suffer other violent acts. The child's parent or guardian is the most common abuser. The National Pediatric Trauma Registry cites that 11 percent, or more than one in ten patients aged 4 and younger, whose records were sent to the registry, were victims of child abuse. And, approximately 95 percent of all pediatric head injuries are caused by child abuse. Child abuse or neglect may result in permanent physical or psychological damage.

More than 40 percent of all head injury deaths and 75 percent of head injuries in general happen to children 14 and younger. Studies cite that 28 percent of abused children had retinal hemorrhaging (bleeding at the back of the eye) compared to 0.05 percent of those with unintentional injuries. And, 13 percent of abused children died compared to 2 percent of non-abused children. Abused children are significantly more likely to need intensive care, and their hospital stays are generally twice as long. They are also four times more likely to die in the hospital compared to children injured in accidents. Frontal lobe injury is highly correlated with impairment of emotional and cognitive expression. Not surprisingly, 96 percent of homicidal children came from chaotic family backgrounds that included violence (81%), family abuse (90%), and learning disabilities (76%). The National Institute of Justice reports that being abused or neglected as a child increases the chances of juvenile arrest by 53 percent and of becoming a violent offender by 38 percent.

Prenatal Drug Exposure

One blind study, utilizing a urine toxicology test, found a 15 percent usage of narcotics in pregnant mothers whose unborn babies were at risk for FAS. Additionally, some pregnant women used over-the-counter medications that were contraindicated during pregnancy. As many as 60 percent of all pregnant women use some medication during pregnancy. This presents a huge risk for the unborn child. Most physicians urge pregnant women to abstain from alcohol, but the message that other drugs (including prescription and over-the-counter medications) are also dangerous needs to be articulated.

It is estimated that about 100,000 babies a year are exposed to prenatal cocaine. Cocaine-exposed infants show signs of toxic exposure similar to the abnormalities that result from in utero exposure to crack, heroin, tobacco, and amphetamines. All pose significant health risks. The degree of disability varies widely depending on the degree of exposure, the timing of it, the comorbidity factors, and the post-natal living environment. Although researchers are still trying to nail down the specific risks of various drugs in various periods of the pregnancy, some evidence indicates that the first trimester is the most crucial period. Fetuses occasionally exposed to light doses of cocaine during the third trimester may achieve normalcy, provided they are raised in a loving and nurturing home and are exposed to no other known toxic factors. However, they remain at higher risk for other problems should they experience any complicating variables.

While early studies failed to find any correlation between maternal crack use and IQ, the tests used evaluated standard intelligence measures only. More recently, studies have indicated that cocaine may damage areas of the brain that regulate arousal, attention, and emotions. These aspects of intelligence, though not measured in standard IQ tests, indeed impact the child's ability to function successfully in the world.

Malnutrition

We know that 25 percent of children in America live in poverty, and that many of these youngsters were undernourished in the womb. Although in malnourished children we see a high prevalence of stunting—an indication of poverty, social deprivation, disease, and resulting cognitive impairment—we also know that the problem extends beyond the conditions of poverty. All socio-economic classes contribute to the problem. It is not atypical, for example, for a middle-class child's diet to consist of too much sugar, starch, and junk food, and not enough nutrients and protein. In fact, more children in America are malnourished than in Angola, Zimbabwe, Cambodia, Haiti, and El Salvador combined.

Iron deficiency is the single most common nutritional disorder worldwide and the cause of anemia during infancy, childhood, and pregnancy. Anemia is linked to short attention span, disruptive behaviors, and impaired memory. It is prevalent in most of the developing world, as well as in the industrialized nations.

Kwashiorkor Syndrome, characterized by retarded growth, changes in skin and hair pigment, edema, and pathologic changes in the liver (including fatty infiltration, necrosis, and fibrosis), is a condition produced by severe protein deficiency. Although first reported in Africa, Kwashiorkor Syndrome is now known throughout the world. Other variations of protein deficiencies, including those seen in some vegans, exist as well. Protein deficiencies have been linked to aggressive behaviors.

Maternal Tobacco Use

Among women 18 to 30 years old, the prime childbearing years, a whopping 38 percent smoke cigarettes. Depending on the specific population sample, the percentage of pregnant women who smoke ranges from 15 to 54 percent! Every year, 50,000 fetal deaths result from smoking during pregnancy; 115,000 miscarriages occur; and 4,000 infant deaths (within 30 days of birth) are attributed to Fetal Tobacco Syndrome (FTS). Smoking accounts for about 25 percent of all low birth weights in the United States.

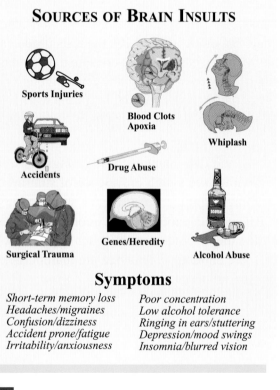

SOURCES OF BRAIN INSULTS

Sports Injuries

Blood Clots
Apoxia

Whiplash

Drug Abuse

Accidents

Genes/Heredity

Surgical Trauma

Alcohol Abuse

Symptoms

Short-term memory loss
Headaches/migraines
Confusion/dizziness
Accident prone/fatigue
Irritability/anxiousness

Poor concentration
Low alcohol tolerance
Ringing in ears/stuttering
Depression/mood swings
Insomnia/blurred vision

The most common disability resulting from fetal tobacco exposure is Attention-Deficit Disorder. However, other significant health, educational, and fiscal implications are associated with FTS as well. It is believed that FTS may increase the risk of childhood leukemia, fetal hypoxia, oral clefts, and respiratory tract infections. It is also correlated with hyperactivity, impulsivity, and learning disorders.

Environmental Toxins

Pesticides, formaldehyde, asbestos, and other toxins contribute to improper brain development. But the most prevalent toxic exposure in children may be lead. Lead poisoning impacts approximately one in twelve boys, primarily those growing up in neighborhoods with exposed pipes, decayed buildings, peeling paint, and high auto emissions. Among 500 boys, the single greatest predictor for delinquency was excess lead exposure. The most common indicator is aggression.

 # COMMENTARY

Although every one of the preceding problems deserves attention, Fetal Alcohol Syndrome is the most pervasive. Much of what we can learn from it also relates to the other conditions that cause developmental and learning delays. In other words, FAS symptoms and the suggested treatments actually form a good guideline for all of the contributing factors of developmental/learning delays.

LD constitutes a moderate to high level of challenge to the classroom teacher. You can contribute to this learner's success, but you will need support from others—notably the parents and learning specialists.

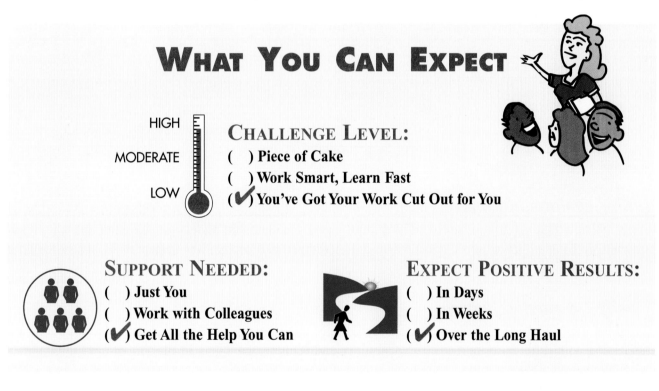

WHAT YOU CAN EXPECT

HIGH
MODERATE
LOW

CHALLENGE LEVEL:
( ) Piece of Cake
( ) Work Smart, Learn Fast
(✔) You've Got Your Work Cut Out for You

SUPPORT NEEDED:
( ) Just You
( ) Work with Colleagues
(✔) Get All the Help You Can

EXPECT POSITIVE RESULTS:
( ) In Days
( ) In Weeks
(✔) Over the Long Haul

 # LIKELY CAUSES

As described previously, there is a host of dominating factors that cause or contribute to learning delays. The less obvious conditions on the following page also represent potential risk factors:

Touch Deprivation

Insufficient infant stimulation through caressing, holding, touching, and massage can result in impaired motivation to learn, emotional adjustment problems, and delayed cognitive development.

Poorly Treated Ear Infections

While ear infections are relatively common among infants, the frequency, severity, and treatment of them are a significant factor in later social and cognitive functioning.

Undiagnosed Deafness or Hearing Impairment

Deaf children from hearing families often do not receive adequate social and linguistic stimulation at an early age. Early detection of deafness and intervention with appropriate linguistic stimulation (i.e., signed language) are necessary to avoid delayed cognitive development. Hearing impairment that is not detected and treated early on can also hinder cognition.

Maternal Personality Disorders

Mothers with narcissistic, paranoid, or histrionic tendencies, or Borderline-Personality Disorder were the least sensitive caregivers. In turn, many of these mothers' babies showed signs of delayed cognitive development at 6 months of age.

Infant Attentional Problems

Infant visual attention can be measured in relation to performance on memory tasks encompassing visual function. Infants that exhibit characteristic prolonged patterns of fixation, appear to be at risk for later cognitive deficits.

Family Interaction Patterns

Variables such as parenting differences (i.e., amount of attention, interaction, and type of interaction) are associated with differences in a child's vocabulary and IQ between 7 and 36 months of age.

Prenatal Toxins

As mentioned earlier, prenatal exposure to alcohol, distress, malnutrition, drugs, and tobacco put children at high risk for physical, cognitive, and social development.

Crowded Living Environments

Studies suggest that parents living in crowded homes speak in less complex, sophisticated ways with their children and are less responsive to them compared to parents in uncrowded homes. Children living in these conditions are also more likely to be abused.

Poor Nutrition

Some studies have shown that infants in developing countries who received supplemental formula (the international standard formulation, known as LCPUFA) had significantly more intentional solutions to problems when compared to a non-supplemented sample of the population. Higher problem-solving scores in infancy are related to higher childhood IQ scores; thus, good nutrition may enhance childhood intelligence.

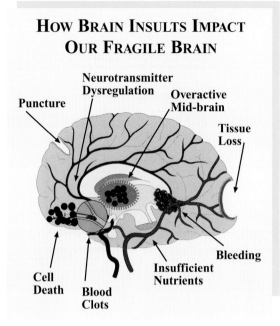

HOW BRAIN INSULTS IMPACT OUR FRAGILE BRAIN

Puncture · Neurotransmitter Dysregulation · Overactive Mid-brain · Tissue Loss · Bleeding · Insufficient Nutrients · Cell Death · Blood Clots

BRAIN AREAS LIKELY INVOLVED

Delayed development is not isolated to a specific area of the brain. Rather, it seems to impact the aggregate, including the following systems:

▼ **Cognitive:** visual-spatial, analytical, mathematical, and creative functioning
▼ **Emotional:** endocrine system, social, cultural, and aesthetic appreciation
▼ **Perceptual-Motor:** listening, vestibular system, sensory acuity, timing, and state management
▼ **Stress Response:** immune response, autonomic nervous system, sympathetic, and parasympathetic nervous systems
▼ **Memory:** listening, attention, concentration

RECOGNIZABLE SYMPTOMS

When a child exhibits consistent behavior or developmental patterns that are different from the norm, pay closer attention and note the nature of the behaviors, preferably on paper. What seems to trigger them? Are they consistent? Are you aware of any extenuating circumstances? Once you've made an effort to

IMPACT OF BRAIN INSULT

SPECT scan
of 15-year-old male
with massive damage
from fall down stairs
at age 18 months.

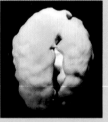

**Top-down view.
Note jagged gap.**

**Underside view. Note
decrease in activity in
several lobes.**

 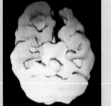

Source: *Images into Human Behavior: A Brain SPECT Atlas*,
Daniel G. Amen, MD, 2000

observe the behaviors, rather than judge them, consider how they might relate to the following characteristics, behaviors, and symptoms:

Fetal Alcohol Syndrome Effects

Size: Growth retardation is below the tenth percentile when corrected for gestational age. These individuals rarely catch up in size, even in an enriched environment.

Central Nervous System: Developmental delays and mild retardation are common; the average IQ is 65 to 85.

Body and Facial Abnormalities: While often subtle, there are some abnormalities that are highly correlated with LD, such as a smaller head, a thinner upper lip, clubfeet, cleft palate, and fingerprint abnormalities. Other abnormalities include small size, low birth weight, retarded growth, smaller eye openings, flat midface, short upturned nose, flat elongated grooves above lip, small chin, and simply formed and low-set ears.

Typical symptoms and behavioral patterns include the following:

▼ **Difficulty structuring work time**
▼ **Impaired rates of learning**
▼ **Poor memory**
▼ **Trouble generalizing behaviors and information**
▼ **Impulsivity**
▼ **Reduced attention span; highly distractible**
▼ **Fearlessness; unresponsive to verbal cautions**
▼ **Poor social judgment**
▼ **Developmental delays in skills like handling simple money transactions**
▼ **Trouble internalizing modeled behaviors**
▼ **Differences in sensory awareness (hypo- or hyper-awareness)**

- ▼ **Language Production higher than comprehension**
- ▼ **Poor problem-solving strategies**
- ▼ **Arithmetic deficits**
- ▼ **Academic functioning averages second- to fourth-grade levels**
- ▼ **Maladaptive behaviors such as poor judgment, distractibility, and difficulty perceiving social cues**

Crack-Exposed Babies

The prevailing myth of *hopeless* "crack babies" is inaccurate. While it is clearly a discouraging and troublesome problem, the following two points indicate reason for optimism: (1) The sheer number of babies born under the influence of crack is small (approximately 4,500 per year) compared to total births; and (2) When provided with a nurturing, enriched environment, most of the symptoms disappear. Unfortunately, most of these children don't receive such an environment.

The degree of disability varies widely in crack-exposed babies depending on the amount of the original exposure, the timing of it, the comorbidity factors, and the post-natal environment. Environmental factors in early childhood seem to intensify or reduce the severity of the symptoms. Crack-exposed children often move from one foster home to the next, have one or no parents, and have inadequate daycare. Typically mothers are poor, white, and single. General symptoms and behaviors in the crack-exposed baby include:

- ▼ **Difficulty processing novel stimuli**
- ▼ **Erratic sleep cycles**
- ▼ **Easily over-aroused and distracted**
- ▼ **Less persistent in task completion**
- ▼ **More aggressive and impulsive**
- ▼ **Easily distressed**
- ▼ **Possibility of speech/language delays**

Studies indicate that the single most predictive factor in the severity of symptoms in crack-exposed babies is the quality of home environment after birth. Unfortunately, most addicted mothers are malnourished, exposed to abuse, living in poor housing, lacking pro-social values, and weak in parental affection. As a result, it's not likely that the birth mothers will sustain a quality, nurturing home environment without intensive intervention/treatment.

Malnutrition

Protein deficiencies can lead to behavior problems. For example, some children perceive hostility where none exists and, therefore, display inappropriate aggression. Anemia (iron shortage) is linked to short attention span, disruptive behaviors, and impaired memory. Lack of B vitamins can lead to impaired thinking and memory.

Anesthesia Exposure

There are some indications that the use of obstetrical anesthesia during delivery may result in subtle alterations in the formation of neurons, synapses, and neural transmitters that are undetectable at birth. In one study, exposed infants/toddlers showed increased probability of delays in typical benchmark developmental tasks such as sitting, standing, and walking. And by age 7, they were more likely to lag in language, judgement, and memory skills.

Environmental Toxins

While there are many potential environmental toxins, lead is the most researched one. Lead exposure has been correlated with aggressiveness, irritability, and short-term memory loss.

Abuse

Typical symptoms and behaviors in the abused child include acting out, shy and anxious behavior patterns, and learning problems. Abuse victims regularly exhibit low frustration tolerance, weak social skills, and low task orientation.

Look for physical signs of abuse, such as unlikely or suspicious bandages, sunglasses worn to hide swelling, or long-sleeved shirts on warm days. Listen for signals of stress in the voice. Abused girls may exhibit abnormally high motor activity or bursts of physical energy. They also may be more resistant to cooperation, more impulsive, and more anxious.

Traumatized children are usually less descriptive and verbal in conversations; they also talk less about themselves and about feelings. They are usually hypervigilant—ever on the look out for potential danger and sensitive to non-verbal cues. Boys generally externalize their exposure to trauma and become more aggressive or isolated. Girls typically internalize the effects by dissociation or simply freezing.

Attachment Disorder

All or most of the following symptoms/behaviors are present in the child suffering from Attachment Disorder.

- ▼ **Manipulative:** superficially engaging or "charming" (a control tactic)
- ▼ **Eye Contact Avoidance:** especially when on parents' terms
- ▼ **Inappropriate Affection:** indiscriminately affectionate with strangers, or, conversely, not inclined to give and receive affection (not cuddly)
- ▼ **Need for Tight Control:** extreme control battles often manifested in covert or "sneaky" ways
- ▼ **Self-Destructive:** also of others, animals, and objects; accident prone; may steal
- ▼ **Hoarding Behavior:** gorging on food and abnormal eating patterns
- ▼ **Preoccupation with Danger:** attracted to fire, blood, and gore
- ▼ **Impulse Control Problems:** cannot internalize cause-and-effect logic; frequently hyperactive; lacking conscience
- ▼ **Developmental Delays:** learning lags and speech disorders common; abnormal speech patterns
- ▼ **Compulsive Lying:** chronically lies even about obvious or crazy things
- ▼ **Weak Social Skills:** poor peer relationships or isolation
- ▼ **Inappropriate Verbal Communication:** persistent nonsense questions and incessant chatter
- ▼ **Demanding:** inappropriately demanding, impatient, and clingy
- ▼ **Parental Hostility:** caretakers likely to appear hostile and angry

WHAT YOU CAN DO

Learn what you can about the particular child in question and the suspected disorder. Talk to parents, school psychologists, counselors, physicians, and other mental-health professionals. Due to the extent and timing of critical neural development, much of the damage is not reversible. While the human brain is highly plastic and malleable, there are limitations. No pharmacological treatment exists presently for children with Fetal Alcohol Syndrome. Those with exposure to milder levels of childhood abuse, blows to the head, and/or other trauma have a much higher treatment success rate than FAS victims. The degree of severity, however, varies a great deal. Don't give up on anyone. Environment plays a crucial role in the future gains of the developmentally-challenged child.

AS AN EDUCATOR

There's a lot you can do! Provide a safe, structured environment with relevant learning activities and high support levels. Do not "dumb down" your class. Rather, incorporate strategies that represent good teaching regardless of special needs. LD students just need *more* high-quality teaching methods on a *more consistent* basis.

Teacher Tips for Managing LD Students

✓ Provide a high level of structure and consistency; routines help learners predict coming events.

✓ Offer a variety of learning activities that utilize multiple learning styles and intelligences.

✓ Keep instructions brief and simple; assign less complex projects to LD students.

✓ Break large projects down into small steps so that learners don't become overwhelmed.

✓ Provide advance notice when an activity shift is going to occur; give learners time to prepare themselves mentally and physically for the change.

✓ Provide plenty of external support structures, such as prompts, written reminders, affirmations, cooperative learning groups, partner sharing, and lists/outlines.

✓ Be concrete when teaching a new concept; show *and* tell *and* give learners hands-on practice.

✓ Be positive. With persistence, some improvement, both cognitively and behaviorally, will occur.

✓ Use rituals; create plenty of predictable events daily in class that make learning fun and exciting.

✓ Get learners' attention through a variety of means, such as music, special guests, and surprises.

✓ Repeat important information numerous times.

✓ Articulate learning goals and objectives repeatedly.

✓ Arrange interventions with specialized training programs and/or tutoring.

✓ Develop a support team of colleagues and professionals to assist you when necessary.

✓ Affirm progress and re-evaluate goals on a regular basis.

✓ Model good stress management practices; take personal time out if necessary, pause and do some deep breathing, and when upsets or setbacks occur, take a different tack.

✓ Strive to build open lines of communication with all learners, but especially the LD student.

✓ Remember, you make a difference.

Be patient in the process. Rome wasn't built in a day. Take note of and appreciate the small miracles that occur on a daily and weekly basis. When upsets and setbacks occur, take in a deep breath and pause. Affirm progress and set new goals. Concentrate on that which you have control over.

AS A PARENT

Parenting a child that is LD or developmentally delayed is undoubtedly a huge challenge; however, it is critical to remember that this is not something the child chose or brought upon themselves. They, above all, need to know they are loved in spite of their condition. As with all children, but especially with the learning delayed, the most important thing you can do is engender in them a sense that (1) they have some control over their lives; (2) what they do is different from who they are; and (3) they are loved despite their condition. With a strong, loving environment, miracles happen everyday. Stay positive.

Testing/Screening

There is good predictive validity for many of the screening devices designed for the early identification of later cognitive delay. Early intervention is essential. Try to rule out potential comorbid disorders such as Attention-Deficit Disorder or depression.

Counseling

Sessions with the school psychologist or other mental-health professionals may be appropriate depending on the type and degree of the learning delay. For most LD children (especially when there are comorbid factors), mediations by a therapist or counselor can help them develop coping skills to better deal with the emotional consequences of their condition.

Nutrition

As a general rule, give your child a daily multi-vitamin and mineral supplement. Make sure they eat a wide variety of food, especially leafy greens, nuts, fruits, and proteins. When LD is a result of brain insults, give your child magnesium and selenium supplements, in addition to the daily multi-vitamin and mineral supplements, to help protect their cells from free radicals. Ensure sufficient intake of vitamins B, C, and E. Reduce high-calcium products (eliminate all dairy from the diet), and avoid iron and iron supplements, aspartame, and MSG.

Behavioral Strategies

✓ Foster independence; encourage self-help and personal problem solving.
✓ Establish a firm routine for bedtime and mealtimes.
✓ Encourage good decision-making; allow some independent decisions.
✓ Focus on teaching daily living skills.
✓ Encourage the use of positive self talk.
✓ Teach children to prepare for school the next day before they go to bed.
✓ Establish a few simple rules. Use identical language to remind them of the rules. For example, "This is your bed; this is where you sleep."

Family Therapy

When a child's developmental delay is (or may be) a result of abuse, both therapeutic and medical attention should be sought for the family. Studies suggest that parental anger and physical discipline/force with children is reduced when families receive cognitive-behavioral therapy. Sometimes abusive parents are prescribed Zoloft, a calming antidepressant. Other antidepressants sometimes prescribed include Paxil, Anafranil, Serzone, Luvox, and Prozac. Blood-pressure medications (i.e., Catapres, Tenex, or Inderal) are sometimes effective in reducing aggressiveness as well. Seek the advice of your health-care professional immediately if abuse is a factor.

Toxins and Allergens from the Environment

Toxins and allergens in the environment can sometimes intensify the problems associated with developmentally-delayed children. If your child has allergic reactions to animal fur, ask your veterinarian about the many available products designed to effectively neutralize animal dander—the true cause of pet allergies. If the problem persists, remove the animal from the house, if possible. If not, do not allow the pet in the child's bedroom and vacuum daily. Mites cannot survive in low temperatures; thus, one way to get rid of them is to occasionally place bed clothes and carpets outside during cold weather. Attend to damp areas in the house where mold can form. Keep lawns mowed down and have old leaves collected on a regular basis by someone other than the affected child. Air cleaners in primary living areas can significantly improve airway hyper-responsiveness in asthmatics. The most common allergy-producing foods are peanuts, milk, eggs, wheat, fish, shellfish, soy, and nuts.

 # MEMORY JOGGER

Remember this face? This is "Miguel," one of the learners introduced in the pre-test at the front of the book. He's also the student who fits the profile for learning delayed. Like the others, Miguel is unique—he exhibits a pattern of symptoms that are associated with a specific disorder. However, some of these symptoms can be observed in other conditions as well. This is why you want to look for *patterns* rather than *isolated behaviors*. To help you remember what's important in assessing LD, take a moment, relax, and focus on the photo, the symptoms, and the key points of this chapter.

Symptoms
- Difficulty structuring work time
- Impaired rates of learning and poor memory
- Has trouble generalizing behaviors and information
- Sometimes exhibits impulsive behavior
- Easily distracted and frequently exhibits reduced attention span
- Displays a sense of fearlessness and is unresponsive to verbal cautions
- Displays poor social judgment
- Has trouble internalizing modeled behaviors
- Language *production* is higher than *comprehension*
- Overall poor problem-solving strategies
- May have unusual facial features

SUPPLEMENTAL RESOURCES

Books

Sensory Integration and Learning Disorders, by Jean Ayers
All Kinds of Minds, by Melvin Levine
Managing Attention and Learning Disorders, by Ian McEwan
Ghosts from the Nursery, Robin Karr-Morse and Meredith Wiley
Shadow Children (about children's learning disorders), by Careth Ellington
The Source for Nonverbal Learning Disorders, by Sue Thompson
Students in Poverty: Toward Awareness, Action, and Wider Knowledge, by the Canadian
   School Boards Association.

Websites

www.cdnsba.org/cmec.html
www.babyzone.com

Organization

National Organization for Fetal Alcohol Syndrome (www.nofas.org)

CHAPTER 6 OUTLINE

The Learner in Motion: Hyperactivity

 ## OVERVIEW

Hyperactivity, in the clinical sense, is a long-term condition persistent beyond age 4 and characterized by chronic restlessness and disruptive behavior. Hyperactive children may continually walk, jump, roll, and fidget. These incessant movements are sometimes disorganized and rapid, but not always; sometimes, they may be slow and measured.

It is important not to confuse hyperactivity with overactivity, a normal childhood behavior exhibited by most children at certain stages of development. Overactivity is not considered hyperactivity unless is persists beyond the age of 4. While hyperactivity is often caused by differences in the learner's brain, overactivity may be a natural response, for example, to an unsuitable learning environment. Educators who still employ a "stand-and-deliver" teaching style are more likely to have students who act out. In contrast, when learners are fully engaged in learning, behavior issues are minimized. Traditional learning environments also require children to sit too long, a developmentally inappropriate expectation. Sitting for extended periods creates postural stress, intensifies restlessness, and reduces oxygen flow to the brain.

Hyperactivity should also not be confused with the more serious condition called Attention-Deficit Disorder (ADD). As described in Chapter One, ADD is a chronic and treatable learning disorder characterized by both impulsivity and time disorientation (achronica). Although hyperactive children may continually be in motion, ADD children exhibit more of an impulsive "stop-start" pattern, as well as other distinct behavior patterns. Hyperactivity is sometimes a component of ADD, but it should not be assumed, as is sometimes done, that the hyperactive child has ADD. These two distinct conditions can be seen in combination in some children. But, clearly, not all hyperactive students have ADD—they simply can't sit still.

 # IMPACT

The impact of hyperactivity on both teachers and students can range from minor to debilitating, depending on the severity of the hyperactivity and the skills of the teacher involved. In classes where the needs of the hyperactive student are ignored, the student can tend to "run the show." However, heavy discipline is not the answer. The hyperactive child is not purposely being obstinate and cannot willfully control the symptoms of his or her condition.

 # DEMOGRAPHICS

Hyperactivity occurs in about 5 percent of children nationwide but increases to 25 percent in selected populations. In students ages 3 to 6, it is true that the hyperactivity component of the traditional Attention Deficit/Hyperactivity combination is often evident. Today's insights, however, tell us that the onset of genuine ADD generally occurs closer to age 6 or 7.

Hyperactivity is most commonly observed in males by a factor of 5-to-1 over females. However, two things should be considered here. First, the majority of elementary-school teachers are women, and many of them may misconstrue typical boy rough-housing, hustling, and exploratory behavior as hyperactivity. Girls are socialized to be quiet and demure, while boys are encouraged to take more risks, play more actively, and use more space. These gender differences are clearly seen during recess when girls typically socialize, and boys more commonly run and engage in other physical activities. This social phenomenon may contribute to the disproportionate number of males diagnosed with hyperactivity.

 # COMMENTARY

Although most children are hyperactive at some point in their development, this is not necessarily cause for alarm. However, by age 4, children should begin to understand when it is more appropriate to sit than stand or walk than run. If a child continues to exhibit hyperactive behavior past this age, the body's regulatory mechanisms may be off kilter, possibly indicating the presence of a disorder.

Keep in mind that there is a continuum of movement possible for all humans. At one extreme is apathy with little or no movement; at the other extreme is hyperactivity. Teachers deal with hyperactivity in different ways. Skilled teachers find ways to adapt without sacrificing the needs of the rest of the class—a task that requires a great deal of awareness, understanding, and flexibility. Adapting to a hyperactive student also requires allowance for more classroom movement and consistent reinforcement of reasonable boundaries.

Hyperactivity poses a low to moderate level of challenge to the classroom teacher. You can definitely contribute to this learner's success!

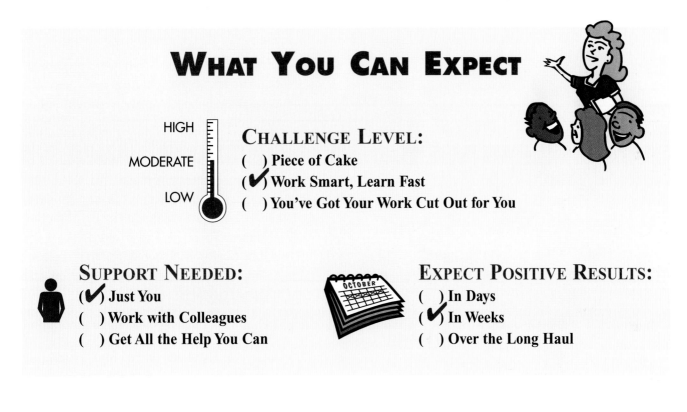

WHAT YOU CAN EXPECT

HIGH
MODERATE
LOW

CHALLENGE LEVEL:
( ) Piece of Cake
(✔) Work Smart, Learn Fast
( ) You've Got Your Work Cut Out for You

SUPPORT NEEDED:
(✔) Just You
( ) Work with Colleagues
( ) Get All the Help You Can

EXPECT POSITIVE RESULTS:
( ) In Days
(✔) In Weeks
( ) Over the Long Haul

? LIKELY CAUSES

Children who are highly kinesthetic (tactile) want to touch, handle, or experience everything first hand. Simply seeing new material or hearing about a subject does not necessarily engage them. Researchers are uncertain exactly how and when each student's learning modality (visual, auditory, or kinesthetic) becomes embedded; however, some speculate that it is internalized between the ages of 3 and 6. For some

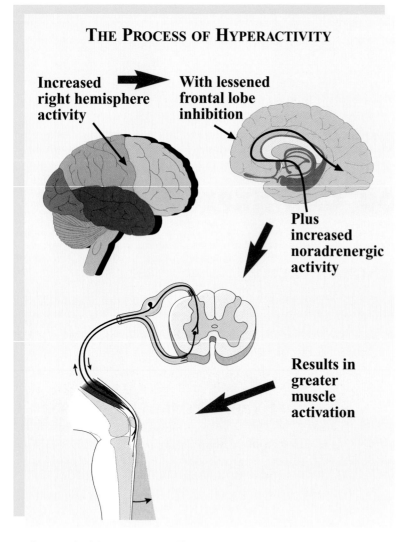

THE PROCESS OF HYPERACTIVITY

Increased right hemisphere activity → **With lessened frontal lobe inhibition**

Plus increased noradrenergic activity

Results in greater muscle activation

reason, more dominant or more numerous pathways in the motor cortex become myelinated in kinesthetic learners, which may, as a result, contribute to hyperactivity.

Chronic Distress

It is clear that chronic exposure to stress, threat, and trauma can affect neurotransmitter levels in the brain. One prominent theory about hyperactivity is that it's caused by an oversupply of adrenaline—the hormone of "urgency." As such, it may trigger the continuous anxious and overactive response seen in the overactive learner. Another theory suggests that dopamine, the "feel good" neurotransmitter, is out of balance in hyperactive children. Thus, they may engage in more novel, exploratory behaviors in an unconscious effort to enhance their mood and obtain a sense of reward.

Nutrition

Many researchers have found that the symptoms of hyperactivity can be lessened with changes in diet. The following dietary habits may contribute to a hyperactive pattern: (1) eating too many of the wrong foods, such as those high in salt, fat, or sugar; (2) not eating enough of the right foods such as green vegetables, nuts, tofu, and other high-protein foods; (3) consuming foods or additives that can cause allergic reactions in some people; and (4) eating sporadically.

Brain Insults

The genuinely hyperactive student may have mild brain damage, but this speculation has been made from a limited number of cases. Because hyperactivity is often seen in combination with other conditions (i.e., emotional disorders, anxiety, recklessness, and aggression), some researchers believe hyperactivity may be the result of brain trauma, seizures, or early attachment deficits.

Heredity

Other theories focus on a genetic component. An increased incidence of hyperactivity in boys whose fathers were hyperactive is evident.

 # BRAIN AREAS LIKELY INVOLVED

Attentional Areas

Two brain systems believed to be involved in hyperactivity are the thalamus and the reticular activating system, which in concert help regulate attention.

Prefrontal Cortex

Also implicated in hyperactivity is the prefrontal cortex, which is important for inhibition of motor responses. This area is underactive in students with persistent hyperactivity.

Motor Areas

The basal ganglia and cerebellum, important to motor activity, are commonly overactive in hyperactive children. The motor-activity system is involved in regulating decision-making, timing, and movement.

OUR ATTENTIONAL SYSTEM

4 What Does This Mean? What Should I Do About It?

3b Focus on New Stimulus

2 Disengage from Current Focus

5 Shut Out Competing Data

3a Reorient

6 Response

1 Sensory Events Activate Attentional System & Sympathetic N.S.

Effector

Sympathetic Nervous System

Spinal Cord

Brainstem

Typically, in hyperactivity an individual's metabolism is markedly reduced in the brainstem and other brain areas partly responsible for regulating attention and motor activity. The neurotransmitter noradrenaline (which also acts as a hormone) is produced at the top of the brainstem. Since this area of the brain is involved in both input and motor regulation, it must be stable to create well-mannered learners.

RECOGNIZABLE SYMPTOMS

In diagnosing hyperactivity, the symptoms must be persistent, but they may vary in type. The following questions should be answered by educators and parents before a diagnosis of hyperactivity is considered: (1) Are the symptoms persistent? (2) Are multiple symptoms present? And, (3) are they impairing the student's ability to learn and socialize? If the answer is yes to all of the above questions, you may have a hyperactive student. The following symptoms are commonly associated with hyperactivity:

▼ **Fidgeting and high need for tactile manipulation**
▼ **Restlessness (standing when others are sitting; running when others are walking)**
▼ **Emotional immaturity**
▼ **Disregarding rules and routines**
▼ **Acting without caution**
▼ **Engaging in occasional antisocial behavior**
▼ **Lessened need to sleep**
▼ **Overdoing simple task**s

WHAT YOU CAN DO

The hyperactive student is not a "wild animal" that needs to be tamed or broken. This applies in the classroom as well as at home. A broken spirit in a child means that nobody wins. Accept and accommodate as best you can the differences in your learners.

AS AN EDUCATOR

First of all, realize that you are not alone in dealing with this issue. Other teachers in your school and thousands of teachers nationwide have hyperactive students. Many of these educators have more than coped; they've thrived. By creating new approaches to accommodate hyperactive students, many teachers have learned to understand, appreciate, and enjoy them.

Maintain a Positive Attitude

Relax and consider that in addition to modifying the hyperactive student's behavior and approaches, you may have to change your own, as well. When your experience with hyperactive students is limited, expect to do some learning. Establish an optimistic attitude and remember that, while the initial knee-jerk response may be to blame the child, this is counterproductive. Just think, if every student were a perfect angel, we wouldn't need as many teachers—and then where would we all be? Developing approaches that are effective with hyperactive students, in the end, makes for better teaching overall.

Employ Movement in the Learning Environment

Think of this as an opportunity to incorporate more movement into your curriculum—a strategy that will positively impact all of your students. Integrate more standing rather than sitting, as well as more walking, more motion, and more hands-on learning activities. At the elementary-school level, a general guideline is to engage learners physically as often as the average age of the students in the class. For example, in a first-grade classroom of 6-year-olds, avoid extending "stand-and-deliver" type instruction for longer than 6 minutes without a physical or hands-on outlet. At the senior-high level, include some movement every 15 minutes or less! Remember that standard classroom chairs are rarely comfortable for more than a few minutes, so appreciate your students' discomfort and need to move. Moving, touching, experimenting, and acting are all strategies that reinforce learning and recall.

Incorporate Skills Training and Emotional Intelligence

Skills training combined with an emphasis on emotional intelligence widens the funnel of learning. To focus solely on academic achievement at the expense of life skills, reduces a learner's opportunities for growth. Teach both. Some educators advocate a theme approach, also known as Thematic Instruction, in which units of study are linked by a common thread. For example, if the theme for the month is "Outer Space," lesson plans might incorporate writing creatively about space, researching a space topic, doing math problems that revolve around a space theme, and holding a "space-race" competition or marathon.

Include "emotional intelligence" skill sets, such as listening skills, conflict-resolution, problem-solving, and relaxation techniques. While it's unlikely you'll experience a complete reversal in behavior, the cumulative effects of a well-planned thematic unit that engages learners should be noticeable over a period of months.

Seek Support/Create a Response Team

If the problem behavior is not resolved over time in spite of your efforts to restructure the environment, involve the parents. It may be that the child needs medical attention. Some children have significant metabolic deficiencies, which you obviously can't correct. Share with parents the strategies you've implemented to accommodate the hyperactivity, including the specific steps you've taken, and the results of those steps. If other accommodations have not resolved the disruptive behavior, the school nurse may be able to help steer parents towards medical treatment.

AS A PARENT

As a parent of a hyperactive child, you will probably see fewer symptoms of the condition than his or her teacher. Chances are you'll notice your child's tendency to fidget more than others his or her age, but because the home environment is usually less restrictive than the classroom, children are less likely to be considered problematic there.

Don't Panic or Try to Stop the Hyperactivity

Rather than trying to stop your child's hyperactivity, focus on channeling his/her energy as much as possible. Hyperactive children need to feel loved and valued in spite of their differences. Does this mean you should overlook inappropriate behaviors? No! In fact, structure is of utmost importance. But do avoid putting conditions on your love. Just because your child is perpetually on the move, does not mean he or she is "broken" or "bad." When hyperactive children learn to structure their time appropriately, they can be highly productive. As with all children, but especially hyperactive ones, the three most important beliefs you can foster are (1) a sense that they have some control over their lives; (2) what they do is different from who they are; and (3) they are loved, despite their condition.

Listen to Your Child and Remain Flexible

If your hyperactive son or daughter complains about their teacher, make an appointment to talk with the teacher and/or school. Some educators do a great job despite the challenges posed by hyperactive students; however, some maintain rigid, outdated behavioral expectations that contribute to, rather than help, the problem. Occasionally, moving a child into another class (presumably where the teacher is more experienced in accommodating hyperactive learners) helps reduce problematic behaviors.

Change the Diet

Sometimes a change in diet positively impacts behavior. Reduce your child's intake of starches, high-sugar carbohydrates, and candy. Add more fruits, nuts, leafy green vegetables, and protein to the diet. Calcium products (i.e., cottage cheese, yogurt, and sesame seeds) can have a calming effect.

Seek Medical Advice

When the problem of hyperactivity persists beyond age 4, it is a good idea to seek psychotherapeutic and/or medical intervention. Although some prescription drugs such as Adderall or Ritalin may be tempting, try alternative measures first.

Know That Your Child Is Not the Problem

Your child is not "broken." Rather, equate the problem to a square peg in a round hole. With thirty kids in a classroom, schools aren't structured for overactive learners. Teachers struggling with how to manage the variables sometimes hold unrealistic expectations. While many children may be able to conform to them, the overactive child may not. When kids are expected to sit for too long, the problem is intensified. Support the process by being consistent with your child at home and reinforcing your rules, the school's rules, and your expectations. Be sure your child's teacher knows you understand the problem and are reinforcing appropriate behaviors, responses, and requests at home.

MEMORY JOGGER

Remember this face? This is "Jeffrey," one of the learners introduced in the pre-test at the front of the book. He's also the student who fits the profile for hyperactivity. Like the others, Jeffrey is unique—he exhibits a pattern of symptoms that are associated with a specific disorder. However, some of these symptoms can be observed in other conditions as well. This is why you want to look for *patterns* rather than *isolated behaviors*. To help you remember what's important in assessing hyperactivity, take a moment, relax, and focus on the photo, the symptoms, and the key points of this chapter.

Symptoms

- Extreme fidgeting; stands instead of sits; walks instead of stands; and runs instead of walks
- Irritability and emotional immaturity
- Ignores routines and rules
- Exhibits continual action; does not use caution
- Constant tactile manipulation
- Often taps, touches, or pushes others

SUPPLEMENTAL RESOURCES

Books

Natural Treatments for Hyperactivity, by Skye Weintraub
If I Could, I Would: A Teenager's Guide to Hyperactivity, by Michael Gordon
Positive Discipline: Teacher's A-Z Guide, by Jane Nelson
Ritalin-Free Kids, by Judyth and Robert Ullman

Websites

www.outsider.co-uk.com
www.campmakebelieve.com
www.zoo-phonics.com
www.mentalhealth.com

7

The Unsound Learner:
Auditory-Processing Deficits

 ## OVERVIEW

A task force of the American Speech, Language, and Hearing Association (ASHA) defines Auditory-Processing Disorder as a deficiency in one or more of the following phenomena: sound localization and lateralization, auditory discrimination, auditory pattern recognition, recognition of temporal aspects of audition, auditory performance decrease with competing acoustic signals, and auditory performance decrease with degraded signals. The terms "central auditory processing" and "auditory processing" are interchangeable, as are the terms auditory perception, central deafness, word deafness, auditory comprehension deficit, and auditory perceptual processing dysfunction.

The factors that influence auditory processing are auditory attention, auditory memory, motivation, maturation and integrity of the auditory pathways, decision processes, and use of linguistic cues such as grammar, meaning in context, and lexical representations. As a result, learners with a central auditory-processing deficit generally are less able to pay attention and follow directions. In addition, they are often hyperactive, easily distracted, and easily frustrated. Organizing and sequencing information presented via the auditory track is also problematic for them.

 ## IMPACT

Speech and language problems are often the earliest indicators of a learning disability. People with developmental speech and language disorders have difficulty producing speech sounds, using spoken language to communicate, or understanding what other people say. The most common auditory subdeficit is Receptive Language Disorder—the inability to understand certain aspects of speech. In this case, the individual's hearing is fine, but they can't make sense of certain sounds, words, or sentences they hear.

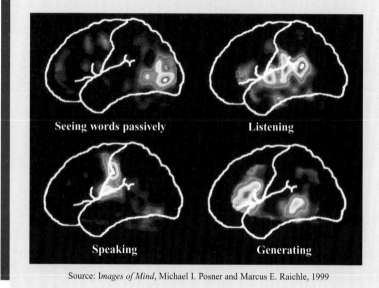

PET Scans Reveal Areas of Brain Activation During Auditory Processing

Seeing words passively

Listening

Speaking

Generating

Source: *Images of Mind*, Michael I. Posner and Marcus E. Raichle, 1999

As a result, they may seem inattentive. As one might also guess, reading disorders are highly correlated with auditory-processing deficits.

Articulation Disorder, another auditory-related problem, is characterized by the inability to control rate of speech and articulate words. These learners may lag behind classmates in learning to make speech sounds. For example, at age 6 the child may say "wabbit" instead of "rabbit" and "thwim" for "swim." Developmental articulation disorders are common. They appear in at least 10 percent of children younger than age 8. Fortunately, articulation disorders are often outgrown or successfully treated with speech therapy. Expressive Language Disorder—a language impairment that is characterized by difficulty expressing oneself in speech—is also common. In this case, the student often calls objects by the wrong names, speaks only in two-word phrases, and/or can't answer simple questions clearly.

DEMOGRAPHICS

The number of learners impacted by auditory-processing deficits (including speech and language disorders) varies depending on the age of the subjects. In general, one out of five (or 20 percent of) children between the ages of 4 and 12 are estimated to have poor phonemic awareness or some kind of auditory-processing difficulty. But, the number drops as the age group increases. For example, in a group of 10-year olds, the number decreases to 7 to 10 percent. The percentage fluctuates also in relation to economic and environmental background, family size, toxic exposure, and geography. By adulthood, the number of individuals still suffering from auditory-processing deficits decreases to 5 to 7 percent.

8

The Out-of-Control Learner:
Conduct Disorder

 ## OVERVIEW

Conduct Disorder (CD) is a severe and chronic, socially-disruptive behavior pattern. It is repetitive and persistent and infringes on the basic rights of others and/or violates major societal norms. Students with CD are *not* the occasional problem learner that disrupt class. Rather, they represent an acute and persistent challenge for teachers.

CD symptoms are sometimes confused with those of other disorders, so ask yourself whether your learner is more like student A or student B described below.

Is This Your Student?
He/she exhibits excessive movement, loud talking, poor classroom manners, weak social skills, and poor posture. He/she teases particular classmates, fails to turn in homework or follow directions, talks out of turn, plays practical jokes, and often dominates classroom agendas.

Or, Is This Your Student?
He/she exhibits inappropriate emotional outbursts, an unwillingness to follow directions or cooperate with others, consistent verbal abuse, and a tendency to swat or hit classmates. He/she challenges authority, uses vulgar language, and intimidates others regularly. Class disruptions, taunting, rudeness, and random acts of destruction are common.

As you may have guessed, Student A is likely seeking attention and/or needs an environmental change. He/she may be acting out in response to an inadequate situation. For example, he/she may be rebelling against an inactive, stale learning environment, too little structure, poor nutrition, poor physical health, or inconsistencies in rules and regulations.

However, student B represents a learner who may have Conduct Disorder. This student clearly needs to be dealt with in a serious fashion. The problem is urgent. Not only is it important to reduce the disruption to other students, but the sanity of the teacher and everyone's safety needs to be considered as well.

 # IMPACT

Chronic physical fighting at the preschool level may indicate severe problems later. If the fighting continues into middle school, there is an 80 percent chance that the student will commit a violent crime. While any behavior problem creates challenges for teachers and other students, Conduct Disorder stretches the patience of all educators. Some evidence suggests that CD is related to the more severe and wide-ranging form of Oppositional Disorder (OPD). Severe OPD, particularly when compounded by other personality disorders, may lead to CD.

CONDUCT DISORDER FACTS

1. The condition is always multicausal.
2. Biology and environment both play a role.
3. The best solution is prevention.

Common Contributing Factors

Heredity
Distress/hypothalamic-pituitary axis
Brain insults/injury
Trauma/Posttraumatic Stress Disorder
Prefrontal cortex dysfunction
Drug/alcohol abuse
Hormonal imbalances
Damaged or immature amygdala
Monoamine imbalances
Lack of social standing/status
Parental abuse/constant threats
Lack of positive role models
Attachment deficit
Lack of conflict resolution skills

 # DEMOGRAPHICS

A 1999 Surgeon General's Report cites that about 10.3 percent of all children have a disruptive conduct disorder—that is 50 students in a school of 500. Although CD is fortunately not as prevalent as some other less serious disorders, it still poses a serious problem in the classroom. As you might guess, there is a far higher incidence of the disorder in males than females. Female behavior disorders are sometimes more difficult to diagnose. Contributing factors may be parental influence and/or paternal genetics. While approximately 45 percent of children with CD have a father who had a disruptive behavior disorder as a youngster, only 20 percent don't have a father with this history. When no risk factors are evident in the father, the likelihood that his child will have CD drops to 5 percent.

Since overlapping neurological systems are involved, children with Attention-Deficit Disorder (ADD) are five times more likely to develop CD by age 12 than those without it. This does not mean that ADD causes CD; it does not. Remember ADD represents an impulse dysregulation problem. Nevertheless, when other factors such as a violent or dysfunctional child-rearing practices are added to the equation, the conditions become ripe for CD. Often parents get frustrated with their ADD children and treat them with scorn, anger, and frustration, which only serves to increase the likelihood of oppositional behaviors. Add years of frustrated teachers, substance abuse, and chronic fighting to the formula, and the incidence of CD increases even more. The rate of disruptive behavior disorders in the children of parental substance abusers is nearly double (36 versus 19 percent) the rate of non-abusers. Even more disturbing is that 84 percent of young murderers (ages 18-24) meet the criteria for CD.

 # COMMENTARY

Children with disruptive behavior disorders, such as CD, have a very difficult time getting along in school. When compared to others, they usually have the worst academic performance records, the poorest relationships, and the weakest self-management skills (taking responsibility, planning, controlling anger, and being punctual).

The issue of safety—a fine thread that distinguishes CD from other behavior problems (including OPD)—is another concern. While children with OPD are an annoyance, they are not especially dangerous. Students suffering from CD, however, tend to raise personal safety concerns for teachers, other students, family members, and/or the sufferer him/herself. If you have a child with CD in your home, most likely you do not feel entirely safe. Or, you do not feel that your things are entirely safe. Some say that CD is the most trying of all pediatric neuropsychiatric disorders for siblings, parents, or caretakers to live with.

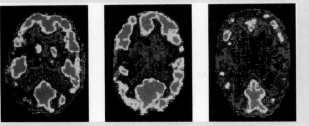

PET Scans Reveal Brain Activations of Homicidal Individuals

View shows prefrontal (top area) activations. On the left is a normal brain with strong activation. The middle brain is a murderer from a deprived environment. The right scan shows strongest frontal dysfunction. Subject is a murderer from a stable home background.

Image Courtesy of Adrian Raine, MD: *Cerebrum.* 1999

Although the challenge level of CD is very high, you can contribute to this learner's success. You will, however, need a great deal of support from others, notably the child's parents, mental-health professionals, and your school administration.

WHAT YOU CAN EXPECT

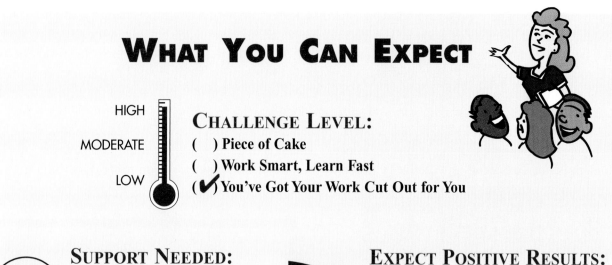

HIGH

MODERATE

LOW

CHALLENGE LEVEL:
( ) Piece of Cake
( ) Work Smart, Learn Fast
(✔) You've Got Your Work Cut Out for You

SUPPORT NEEDED:
( ) Just You
( ) Work with Colleagues
(✔) Get All the Help You Can

EXPECT POSITIVE RESULTS:
( ) In Days
( ) In Weeks
(✔) Over the Long Haul

❓ LIKELY CAUSES

It is not known for sure what causes CD, but the following represent probable contributing factors:

Chemical Dysregulation

One cause (or symptom) of CD may be chronically low levels of cortisol and/or related neurotransmitters. For 4 years, researchers followed 38 boys who had been referred to a psychiatric clinic for disruptive behavior. Subjects with a consistently lower-than-average cortisol level exhibited antisocial behavior at a younger age; they exhibited three times the number of aggressive symptoms; and they were three times as likely as subjects who had higher (or fluctuating) cortisol concentrations to be identified as mean or combative by their classmates. Cortisol is secreted in response to stressful or threatening situations. Low levels may influence how these young males respond to potential stressors. Boys with consistently lower cortisol levels seem to be unafraid of retribution. It is possible that since they don't feel stress in the same way, they don't develop the typical coping strategies, like avoidance.

Reduced Prefrontal Activity

A study conducted by The University of Southern California and The University of California, Irvine compared the brain scans of 38 men and women charged with murder to those of 26 subjects considered "from benign backgrounds." The individuals from benign backgrounds averaged 5.7 percent less activity in the medial prefrontal cortex. More significantly, a specific area of the medial prefrontal cortex—the orbitofrontal cortex on the right hemisphere—showed 14.2 percent less activity. This is significant when you consider that the prefrontal cortex inhibits aggressive behavior.

This finding suggests that individuals with CD may have experienced abnormal neurological development before or after birth. The differences in brain activity could not be explained by other factors, such as age, gender, ethnicity, handedness, Schizophrenia, or generalized brain dysfunction. Another theory is that delivery complications at birth may cause neurological vulnerabilities (or brain insults) that contribute to the problem. Some evidence indicates that CD, in addition to a combination of OPD with ADD or a mood disorder, arises from similar cortical-subcortical loops.

BRAIN ACTIVATION IN NORMAL AND VIOLENT SUBJECTS

The PET scan on the left is a normal control subject with strong prefrontal activation. The PET scan of a murderer on the right shows diminished yellow and red activation at the top of the brain, suggesting diminished capacity to inhibit irrational, violent thoughts.

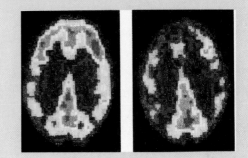

Image Courtesy of Adrian Raine, MD: *Cerebrum.* 1999

Abuse/Family Environment

Parents who are physically abusive and/or highly critical and hostile are more likely to have poorly adjusted children that exhibit behavior problems at school and home. These children also have more trouble establishing good relationships with their peers, teachers, and family members. When a parent is abusing drugs or is depressed, they are less responsive to their child's needs. The first 18 months of a child's life are particularly critical to the attachment and attunement process.

Children learn what's modeled for them. A child who consistently receives negative responses to social and emotional encounters with their primary caregiver(s) learns that people cannot be relied upon, and he/she ultimately disconnects. In an abusive environment, they learn that the way to get their needs met is to be aggressive and/or violent.

Maltreatment (especially of girls) represents a significant risk factor for numerous other subsequent psychiatric conditions and behaviors beyond Conduct Disorder, including Borderline Personality Disorder, Antisocial Personality Disorder, Posttraumatic Stress Disorder (Syndrome), eating disorders, dissociative disorders, substance abuse, Somatization Disorder, suicide, depression, and self-mutilation.

Trauma

Early loss experiences may alter brain function in a way that renders the individual more susceptible to subsequent environmental stressors. In persons genetically predisposed to a disorder such as major depression, this could be a crucial factor in bringing any genetic predisposition to the fore.

Parental Substance Abuse

Abnormal fetal development due to maternal substance abuse and/or smoking during or before pregnancy may lead to subtle damaging effects on brain regions that control attention and movement.

Poor Parenting Skills

Dr. Gerry Patterson of the Oregon Social Learning Center cites seven random trials he's conducted as evidence that parenting skills are at the core of disruptive behavior disorders. In response, he developed a month-long program called "First Steps" as an intervention for children 4 to 6 years old. The program, which is successful in 50 percent of cases, combines pro-social skills training for children with positive parenting skills for primary caretakers. In spite of this, a more widely accepted theory is that weak parenting skills *combined* with brain-based origins set the stage for CD.

 # BRAIN AREAS LIKELY INVOLVED

Frontal Lobes

This area of the brain (including the medial prefrontal cortex to a moderate degree and the orbitofrontal cortex on the right hemisphere to a more significant degree) is highly involved with inhibition and impulsiveness.

Midbrain

This area of the brain (including the hypothalamus all the way to the adrenals) is highly involved in the secretion of cortisol.

Amygdala

This area of the brain is responsible for intense emotions, such as rage. In CD, it may be hypersensitive to threat and distress, evoking more reactive impulses.

Genes

A strong genetic component is indicated. While we're not likely born with the disorder, one may be born with a temperament and chemistry that favors the possibility of developing the disorder.

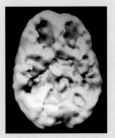
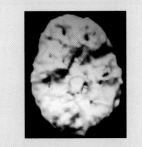

SPECT SCAN OF TEMPORAL AND PREFRONTAL LOBE ACTIVITY IN VIOLENT SUBJECTS

A SPECT scan of the underside of the brain. Note top right area. This violent 9-year-old boy has a cyst in the left temporal lobe which contributes to temper dysfunction and uncontrolled outbursts.

SPECT scan of underside of brain of violent male showing decreased prefrontal and temporal lobe activity.

Source: *Images into Human Behavior: A Brain SPECT Atlas,*
Daniel G. Amen, MD, 2000

RECOGNIZABLE SYMPTOMS

CD elicits many opportunities for misdiagnosis. Be careful not to mistake it for more common "look-alike" conditions that are far *less* serious. Although the following symptoms don't necessarily equate to Conduct Disorder, they are sometimes present:

▼ A lack of standard social skills, such as greeting skills, maintaining a conversation, listening, behaving in a socially-acceptable manner, and/or taking into account the needs of others. At the more extreme level, sufferers may be unable to form or maintain close relationships or resolve interpersonal problems.

▼ Mood disorders, such as anxiety or depression.

▼ Hyperactivity as defined by excess motor activity such as squirming, fidgeting, or pacing. Manifestations can be age-related (little kids might do a lot of extra running, climbing, jumping; whereas, a hyperactive 18-year-old would be more likely to display excess fidgeting).

▼ Impulsivity or the tendency to make snap decisions and act upon them with disregard to consequences. Impulsivity is also characteristic of Attention-Deficit Disorder. It becomes a problem when the frequency is high and/or the consequences harmful.

▼ Adolescent antisocial behaviors that aren't accounted for by other disorders.

If sudden onset occurs, suspect other possibilities. If, however, a student exhibits consistent chronic disruptive behavior patterns that aren't diagnosed as other disorders, suspect CD. One symptom is not enough, but two or more, exhibited consistently over a period of months is cause for further investigation. Watch and listen for the following additional symptoms:

▼ Aggressive and disruptive behavior patterns (can start as early as first grade). Such behavior is considered an antecedent (or predictor) of teenage delinquency.
▼ Inappropriate emotional outbursts, including random acts of destruction.
▼ Consistently hurtful towards others, such as intimidating, swatting, and/or hitting others.
▼ Refuses to follow directions and directly challenges authority.
▼ Loud and consistent verbal abuse of others, including taunting the teacher, lying, and using vulgar language.
▼ Unwillingness to participate with others socially.

The student with CD may be physically cruel to people and animals, have little or no regard for others' feelings, and exhibit a high incidence of lying, stealing, and peer aggression. Often the sufferer has a misperception that others are threatening him/her when they're not. CD sufferers may be chronic bullies, even fighting with weapons. They fail to link up cause and effect—for example, lying and then not understanding why you don't trust them. They steal without a conscience; they blame others for their troubles; and they cannot acknowledge other people's perspective because the only view that exists for them is their own. Since they experience the world as outside of their control, anything bad is someone else's fault.

 # WHAT YOU CAN DO

Early intervention is critical. CD can be evident as early as 3 or 4 years of age and, in some cases, even as early as 2. The age to intervene is before kindergarten, not when the child has later become a juvenile offender. When you observe the signs of CD over a period of months, it's time for a strong intervention. Do not lock horns with the sufferer; you will lose. In their mind, they're always right. They feel little or no guilt and no social conscience. There are things you can do, however, to accommodate the situation. Here are some suggestions:

AS AN EDUCATOR

This is a serious disorder with significant consequences. Do not attempt to treat a child suspected to be suffering from CD alone. Get help! A response team approach is essential. Involve parents, school administrators, mental-health professionals, and sometimes the student him/herself. Move quickly on this issue.

Remember that this student's brain is disordered. You'll need to be smart. Often individuals with CD play the blame game and convince people around them that another party is causing the problem. These individuals may come across as smart and believable, but they are generally highly manipulative personalities. Their blame game works brilliantly to keep concerned individuals off balance. As various parties begin to suspect each other of mistreating the CD student, progress is stalled. You'll need a united front. Sometimes it helps to get school administrators, psychiatrists, parole officers, parents, and teachers to sit down together and talk so the student cannot play one person or group off another.

Organize a Response Team

✓ Set a time to meet regularly with the response team.
✓ Make it a practice not to rely on information from the sufferer that is unchecked and/or not confirmed.
✓ Do not include the student in these discussions.
✓ Do, however, subsequently share with the student the plan established in the meeting.
✓ Consider both psychological (behavior modification) and physical (drug therapy) interventions when devising the plan. Seek professional medical advice.
✓ Always include emotional intelligence skills in your curriculum. Teens who participated in a behavior management intervention in first grade were significantly *less likely* than non-participants to start smoking or to engage in antisocial behavior during middle school.

Develop a Plan

With the help of the response team, devise a plan for dealing with the learner's disruptive behavior patterns. With a plan in place, you're less likely to overreact or be sucked into the learner's emotional whirlpool. You don't want to intensify the situation; rather, your goal ought to be to maintain consistent expectations and to de-escalate problem situations when they occur. The following relevant questions ought to be asked by the team: What response is appropriate when the student disrupts class or incessantly annoys others? What response is appropriate when the student gets into a fight? What if he/she brings a weapon to school? What should we do when he/she throws a major temper tantrum? What response is called for if the student verbally threatens to commit suicide, hurt others, or run away? For the plan to work, however, other agreements, like the following, need to be made as well.

Don't Assume the Sufferer Is Being Truthful

Individuals suffering from CD consistently lie. Do not buy into their stories without substantial corroborated evidence.

Be Specific with Requests

Select only one or two specific inappropriate behaviors that you wish to target. Rather than requesting the learner to "be good," try "follow my directions please."

Be Consistent

It is important that the youngster with CD not receive mixed messages from school and home or from different care providers. Make sure everyone is "on board" with the plan and that they are using it appropriately.

Grant Privileges Rather than Rewards

When using a behavior-modification approach (based on rewards and punishment), use privileges to reinforce appropriate behaviors, rather than monetary or object rewards.

Share the Plan with the Individual

The plan should be simple and straightforward so that your student can easily understand it. If the student can read, he/she should have a written copy of it. If appropriate for the age, have the student sign an agreement or "behavior contract."

Seek Professional Advice

A "behavior contract" alone is not the treatment answer for this serious disorder. Strong intervention at home is also needed. Family therapy with a psychologist or psychiatrist can be useful in improving parent/child dynamics. A psychiatrist may also prescribe drug therapy if she/he deems it necessary. This is a serious disorder that cannot be alleviated by a few kind words.

Strive for Early Detection

Stay alert to patterns that may indicate a problem (such as chronic fighting). If you ignore the symptoms and signs, a child's silent plea for help goes unheard. Instead, document the problems as they arise. Cite the specifics of the event (i.e., date, time, behavior, response, and any extenuating circumstances) in a notebook or journal. If the learner's behavior continues to be persistently inappropriate, even after you've set down clear expectations and ground rules, notify parents and the school counselor. Interventions are far more effective when administered in third or fourth grade versus high school.

AS A PARENT

Pay close attention to your child's developmental stages. Clues that the child may have CD are, in some cases, evident as early as age 2 or 3! Some parents comment that their children just didn't "hook in" to normal interactions with others. Some remark that their child hardly ever walked—that he/she just started running everywhere. Others say their child avoided eye contact. Act early on such cues to avoid more difficult problems later on.

Move Forward Quickly

Once you notice a problem, take it seriously. Ignoring it will not make it go away. In fact, it will make it worse. Left untreated, most children with CD suffer tremendous repercussions, including academic and social failure. Don't let guilt about what you did or didn't do in the past stop you from getting the

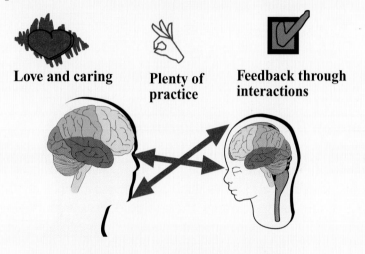

PARENT/INFANT INTERACTION AND ATTUNEMENT

During the first 18 months of life, infant attunement with parents is essential for emotional and social attachment.

Love and caring   **Plenty of practice**   **Feedback through interactions**

Attunement involves back-and-forth games, storytelling, and brief caregiver interactions. Abuse, neglect, or misattunement may lead to overpruning of synapses in the right prefrontal cortex, causing later inability to modulate emotions. Often, this results in hurting others without thinking and feeling any remorse.

appropriate treatment for your child now. Focus on the task at hand. Show your child that they are loved and valued in spite of what they do or don't do. Does this mean overlooking inappropriate behaviors? No. You can both love your child and consistently enforce appropriate rules and expectations. In the end, the most important objective is to help your child feel confident despite of his/her condition.

CD SUFFERERS ARE BEST HELPED BY PARENTS WHO TRY TO FOSTER IN THEIR CHILD...

▼ A sense of control over their lives.
▼ A sense that *what they do* is different from *who they are*.
▼ A feeling that they are loved despite their condition.

Employ Behavior Management

A behavioral approach focuses on reinforcing appropriate behaviors first, so that the CD sufferer can function in the world. This approach usually includes both counseling and a behavior-management plan implemented by all parties that serve as caregivers. The emphasis of the plan should be on setting and maintaining limits, learning effective responses, maintaining stability, and creating an emotionally calm environment. The same criteria as outlined for educators apply to parents as well, such as meeting regularly with the response team, fact-checking information supplied by the CD sufferer, and maintaining a unified and consistent front with other caregivers.

Strengthen Parenting Skills

An unusual problem demands unusual answers. Do not assume you can deal with this problem alone. Get help. The disruptive behavior patterns exhibited by the CD sufferer are difficult to deal with as a parent. Learn *what* to say, *when* to say it, and *how* to say it so that you and your child don't fall into a vicious downward spiral. Many parents find the additional support of a good counselor and a parenting group essential.

Expect the Unexpected

As with many of the other disorders discussed thus far, CD frequently represents only a piece of the puzzle. Comorbidity is common. Aside from being prone to other overlapping disorders, the CD sufferer is also at higher risk for drug and alcohol abuse. Keep your eyes and ears open for clues that may indicate other problems.

Seek Medical Advice

Zoloft, which is a drug commonly prescribed for depression, is also used to treat Conduct Disorder. Other options include Paxil, Anafranil, Serzone, Luvox, and Prozac. These medications are usually effective in reducing disruptive behaviors; however, side effects are common. Learn about the various medications and their potential side effects; then, be prepared for a period during which the most effective medication for the individual is identified through trial and error.

Blood pressure medications such as Catapres, Tenex, or Inderal are also sometimes used to treat very aggressive children and adolescents who rarely sleep. This option has been shown to be safe even in the treatment of very young children (i.e., preschool-age). Dixarit is a child-friendly version of this class of drugs. It is sweet tasting and looks like the popular candy called Smarties, so it is easier to administer. However, depression—a problematic side effect of this medication—occurs in about 5 to 10 percent of patients who take this drug. Medications of this sort, therefore, need to be monitored by a physician (and you) very closely.

Take a Comprehensive Approach

Medication alone is not the answer. A combined approach that includes behavior therapy and other treatment options is usually most effective. Seek support; present a united front; and take the disorder seriously. Parental involvement is key.

Remember this face? This is "Joshua," one of the learners introduced in the pre-test at the front of the book. He's also the student who fits the profile for Conduct Disorder. Like the others, Joshua is unique—he exhibits a pattern of symptoms that are associated with a specific disorder. However, some of these symptoms can be observed in other conditions as well. This is why you want to look for *patterns* rather than *isolated behaviors*. To help you remember what's important in assessing CD, take a moment, relax, and focus on the photo, the symptoms, and the key points of this chapter.

Symptoms

- Inappropriate emotional outbursts with random acts of destruction
- Consistently hurtful towards peers—swatting, hitting, and verbal intimidation
- Refuses to follow directions directly; consistently challenges authority
- Loud and aggressive communication patterns, often taunting the teacher and using vulgar language
- Unwilling to participate with others in normal social activities
- Is prone to lie

SUPPLEMENTAL RESOURCES

Books

Conduct Disorders: The Latest Assessment and Treatment, by Mark Eddy
Disruptive Behavior Disorders in Children, by Elizabeth Conneley
Savage Spawn: Reflections on Violent Children, by Johnathan Kellerman
The Biology of Violence, by Debra Niehoff
Change Your Brain, Change Your Life, by Daniel G. Amen, MD
Ghosts from the Nursery, by Robin Karr-Morse and Meredith Wiley

Websites

www.mentalhealth.com *(Internet Mental Health)*

Organizations

American Academy of Child and Adolescent Psychiatry (www.aacap.org)

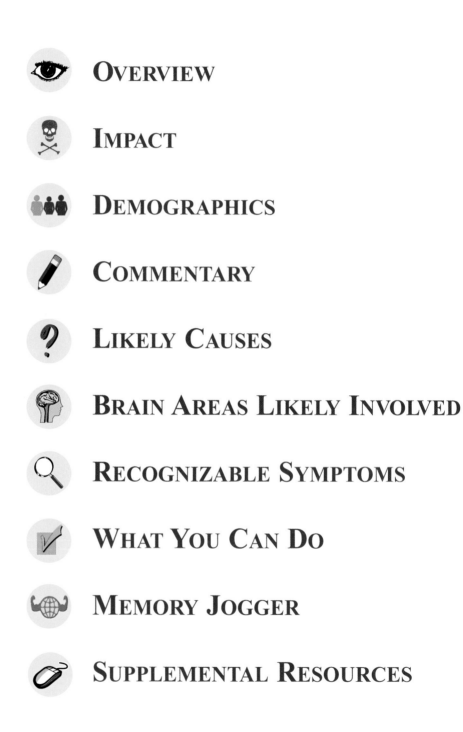

9

The Demotivated Learner:
Chronic Threat and Distress

 ## OVERVIEW

The most common cause of academic demotivation is chronic exposure to distress and/or threat. These conditions can dwell in most environments, including home, community, and school. Distress can be physical or emotional. It can be a result of something mundane like long-term irrelevant curriculum, sedentary instruction, or teaching/learning style mismatches. Or, it can be the result of something more intense like abuse, hunger, and peer violence. School for many students is a dangerous place. And when perceived so, a learner's instinct to survive overrides the motivation for academic success. When this evolutionary response to threat or distress occurs time after time, the learner's brain ultimately suffers. Eventually a maladaptive response to even everyday stressors may result.

While moderate short-term stress, in most cases, is conducive to learning and a healthy immune response, chronic distress is debilitating. And, unfortunately, children are not spared from this rule. It is true that we have a fault-tolerant brain, and, most of the time, we adapt well to daily stress; however, when stress-related hormones (known as glucocorticoids) are chronically elevated, learners can become distracted, hurried, apathetic, ditsy, and uninterested in learning. Recent neuroscientific research confirms that, when these excess glucocorticoids are present over an extended period of time, brain cells ultimately die and aging is accelerated.

Understanding Threat

No longer do saber-toothed tigers threaten our lives; however, the academic equivalent lives on. It may be in the form of the playground bully, an abusive parent, or even a teacher who embarrasses students in front of their peers. Threat is an acute state of alarm characterized by some risk and urgency. Threatening occurrences can be divided into two categories: (1) "primary activation" (a real or immediate threat); and (2) "reactivation" (a remembered or potential threat).

Primary activation in the classroom setting can occur when a teacher calls on an unprepared student or when a student has to present in front of his/her peers with insufficient preparation. It can also occur in an abusive household, on the way to school, on the playground, or anywhere danger is present.

While some neuroscientists, like Joseph LeDoux, believe that the brain's threat system is activated like an "on-off" switch, others, like Paul Whalen, have demonstrated that it works more like a rheostat. Everyone, however, agrees that when threat is perceived, the body prepares itself with a bath of glucocorticoids, among them adrenaline (the fight or flight hormone), in an effort to protect itself.

Reactivation occurs when a prior activation of threat or distress is triggered. This can happen in any environment, including a truly safe one. The mere sound of a ruler hitting the desk or the sight of a grade-book, for example, can reactivate a prior intense negative association, triggering the stress response. When this occurs, the amygdala, a midbrain area highly involved in memory and emotion, "recreates" the past in our mind. We all have triggers that can set us off.

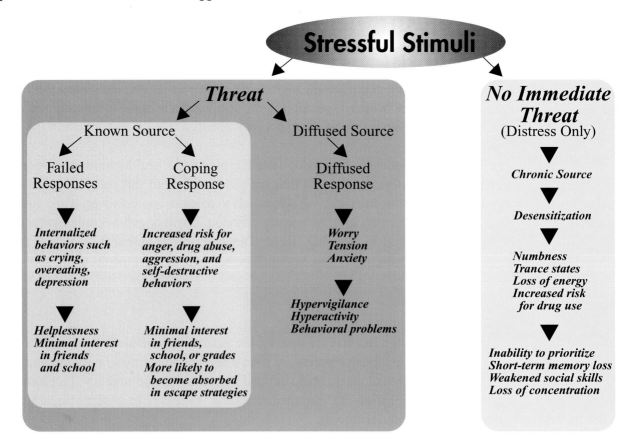

Understanding Distress

Distress is a chronic condition characterized by the release of excess glucocorticoids, including cortisol, the hormone of negative expectations. While in the short run cortisol can be beneficial, over the long haul, elevated levels wreak havoc on the human body. Though not usually life threatening, distress can impair learning. Distress has been categorized and explained in the following ways:

Short-term trauma or a single discrete traumatic event, such as the violent death of a school acquaintance, can result in short-term dysfunction in individuals who are otherwise healthy. Common effects include intense bad memories or dreams, emotional numbing, feelings of detachment or unreality, and bodily tension. The victims of short-term trauma usually experience a complete recovery within weeks of the occurrence.

Acute Stress Disorder is a short-term condition (less than a month) generated by an unusually traumatic event that provokes fear, horror, or helplessness, and causes emotional numbing, hyperarousal, severe anxiety, and distressing dreams or recollections of the experience. Like the more chronic condition, Posttraumatic Stress Disorder (or Syndrome), Acute Stress Disorder is often seen in soldiers returning from combat, but it is also prevalent in civilians, including children. It can be caused, for example, by a catastrophic natural disaster such as a fire, earthquake, or tornado or by physical violence such as a rape, robbery, kidnapping, shooting, bombing, or gang activity. The condition is characterized by panic reactions, mental confusion, dissociation, severe insomnia, suspiciousness, and an inability to manage even basic self-care, work, and social activities. If the symptoms last longer than one month, a diagnosis of Posttraumatic Stress Disorder (PTSD) might be indicated.

Posttraumatic Stress Disorder (PTSD) is the chronic version of Acute Stress Disorder. The two conditions share the same criteria for diagnosis, except that PTSD symptoms extend beyond a month. PTSD is also caused by severe trauma due, for example, to a natural or man-made disaster and is characterized by persistent re-experiencing of the traumatic event, avoidance of stimuli associated with the trauma, emotional numbing, and hyperarousal or severe anxiety. The condition may overlap with one or more other psychiatric disorders such as depression, alcohol/substance abuse, Panic Disorder, and/or other anxiety disorders. The most extreme cases are referred to as Complex PTSD or "Disorder of Extreme Stress." Complex PTSD is generally seen in individuals who have been exposed to prolonged trauma, especially during childhood, such as repeated childhood sexual abuse. These individuals are often also diagnosed with other serious psychiatric conditions such as a dissociative disorder, Borderline Personality Disorder, or Antisocial Personality Disorder. The behavioral difficulties they may experience include impulsivity, aggression, sexual acting out, eating or sleeping dysfunction, alcohol/drug abuse, and/or other self-destructive actions. Extreme emotional difficulties (such as intense rage, depression, or panic) and mental difficulties (such as fragmented thoughts, dissociation, and amnesia) are also prevalent.

 # IMPACT

The single hardest hit group of trauma victims is children. As these children enter adolescence and adulthood, the symptoms resulting from the trauma are often amplified by additional trauma. Potential threats are many and varied. They may stem from abusive parents, violent neighborhoods, inadequate child care, chronic incidents of bullying in transit to school or at school, unsafe school environments, or even a single abusive classmate.

PTSD was originally diagnosed in combat veterans. It is also seen in a disproportionate number of rape and incest victims, survivors of natural or man-made disasters, and witnesses of extreme violence. The statistics generally show that about 30 percent of people who experience temporary traumas develop PTSD. However, the number rises steeply to 80 or 90 percent in victims of repeated or chronic trauma. People with PTSD often exhibit other psychological difficulties, as well—particularly depression, substance abuse, or an anxiety disorder. Treatment success increases when comorbid conditions are appropriately diagnosed and treated first (or in conjunction) with PTSD.

 # DEMOGRAPHICS

More than a million children in this country alone are exposed to the type of threat and distress that can lead to PTSD. In fact, 10 percent of the American population has been affected at some point by clinically diagnosable PTSD. And, about 4 percent of the population will experience symptoms of PTSD in a given year. PTSD can occur at any age. Not every traumatized person, of course, experiences PTSD; however, we do know that in non-combat situations, PTSD affects both genders with a higher incidence reported in females. In animal models, interestingly, the *more* outgoing and aggressive the rats, the *more* likely they were to experience threat and distress.

 # COMMENTARY

An important myth to dispel is that PTSD and Acute Stress Disorder only occur in war veterans. In fact, children are the largest group impacted. Symptoms are usually evident within 3 months of the trauma; however, onset sometimes doesn't occur until years later. The course of the illness varies. Some people recover within 6 months; others have a longer battle. In some cases, the condition may be chronic.

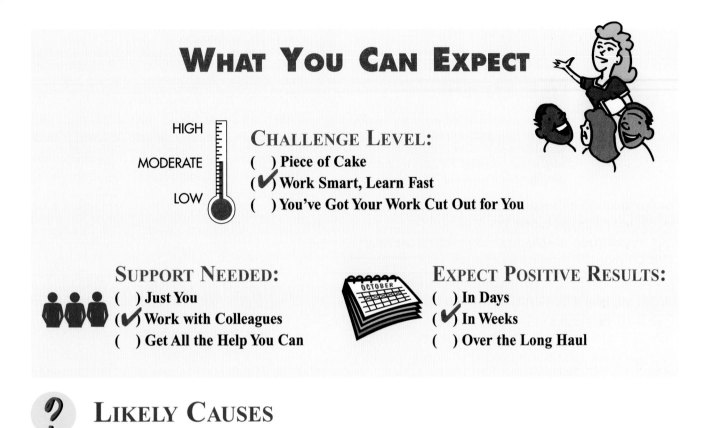

WHAT YOU CAN EXPECT

CHALLENGE LEVEL:
( ) Piece of Cake
(✔) Work Smart, Learn Fast
( ) You've Got Your Work Cut Out for You

HIGH
MODERATE
LOW

SUPPORT NEEDED:
( ) Just You
(✔) Work with Colleagues
( ) Get All the Help You Can

EXPECT POSITIVE RESULTS:
( ) In Days
(✔) In Weeks
( ) Over the Long Haul

❓ LIKELY CAUSES

Traumatic Environmental Conditions

Traumatic conditions, especially early in a child's life, can profoundly impact personality. When internalized and reinforced, these events remain forever painful and present. Early parental loss, for example, accompanied by the lack of a supportive relationship subsequent to the loss (an external stress-reducing factor), could easily set off a series of circumstances that ultimately result in Acute Stress Disorder or PTSD. Other traumatic environmental conditions include a poverty cycle, abandonment, abduction, emotional, sexual, and/or physical abuse, parental fighting, feeling trapped in an unhappy marriage or in a despised job or career, political violence, and ethnic rivalries. With no hope, the individual eventually gives up searching for solutions.

Prenatal Distress

Some non-human research indicates that prenatal stress may predispose infants to having a more difficult temperament pattern. Attentional disorders, neuromotor deficits, diminished cognition, and fewer play behaviors may be evidenced.

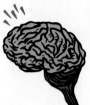

Abuse & the Brain

1. All socio-economic classes are at risk.
2. Two to four million children per year are abused.
3. Up to one-third of all girls/women are/have been abused.

Symptoms are age dependent

- Burns and bruises visible
- Weakened short- and long-term memory
- Unusual limps or slowness
- Extremes of aggression and withdrawal
- Overloaded, often "freezing up"
- Extremes of emotions
- Hypervigilance, stress disorders
- Anxiety and increased startle response

Unsafe Schools

Many schools are simply not safe for children. Metal detectors and on-site security officers do not create the feeling of safety. Rather, they can trigger the threat response. A sense of safety is better generated by a school-wide commitment to the caring, nurturing, and acceptance of children. It is generated by teachers who have a zero tolerance policy for threats of any kind. It is fostered by administrators who make a threat-free school their top priority.

High Resting Heart Rate

Significant cardiovascular liability is a prominent feature in children with PTSD. A sample of children with PTSD reveals that about 85 percent of them have a high resting heart rate—greater than 94 beats per minute, and about 40 percent have resting rates greater than 100 beats per minute. An age-comparable group of normal children exhibits an average resting heart rate of 84 beats per minute.

Frontal-Lobe Dysfunction

It is common for people experiencing acute stress to be overly aroused, short-tempered, irritable, anxious, and tense. They cannot prioritize their schedule: They cannot tell the difference between important and unimportant objectives or urgent and non-urgent situations. Without a way to prioritize, they become victims. They take on too much, have too many irons in the fire, and can't organize the slew of self-inflicted demands and pressures clamoring for their attention. These choices are all functions of the executive decision-making area of the frontal lobe.

Distortion

A distorted belief system or view of the world can cause unending stress for an individual (i.e., "The world is a threatening place." "People will find out I'm a pretender." "We have to be perfect at all times.").

BRAIN AREAS LIKELY INVOLVED

Autonomic Nervous System

Our brain directs both our sympathetic system (in emergency conditions) and our parasympathetic system (in normal conditions). Both of these implicit systems activate and suppress bodily functions that help us respond appropriately to life. Chronic threat and distress, however, can ultimately alter the healthy functioning of our sympathetic systems. The source of the problem is not a busy, stressful life, but our capacity to remember and create. The overstimulation that occurs in response to dozens of feared or imagined future events further complicates the ability to separate genuine from illusory threats.

Hypothalamus

Our response to distress starts here. When the hypothalamus is activated, messages travel through the brain, down the spinal cord, and out to our cells, glands, skin, and muscles. The messages are conveyed through axons that project from spinal cord cells. This process is activated by the hormone corticotropin-releasing factor (CRF), which stimulates the pituitary gland to release adrenocorticotropin hormone (ACTH). These hormones cause the adrenal glands to secrete hormones that stoke the stress response—indicated by an increase in anxiety, blood pressure, energy, and suppression of immune responses.

In response to distress, the adrenal glands secrete two primary chemicals. Epinephrine (adrenaline) acts within seconds but cannot be sustained, while glucocorticoids (steroid hormones) last for minutes, hours, or days, but aren't activated as quickly. These biochemical responses to threat also stimulate the pancreas to release its own hormone, glucagon, which provides the sustained energy necessary to deal with the stress.

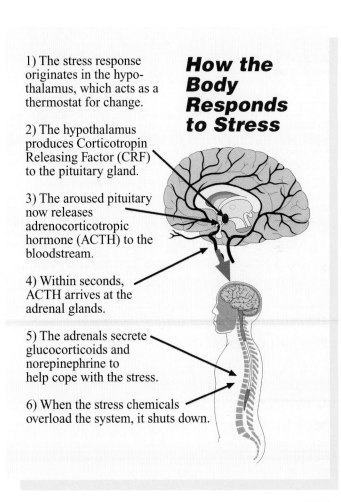

1) The stress response originates in the hypothalamus, which acts as a thermostat for change.

2) The hypothalamus produces Corticotropin Releasing Factor (CRF) to the pituitary gland.

3) The aroused pituitary now releases adrenocorticotropic hormone (ACTH) to the bloodstream.

4) Within seconds, ACTH arrives at the adrenal glands.

5) The adrenals secrete glucocorticoids and norepinephrine to help cope with the stress.

6) When the stress chemicals overload the system, it shuts down.

How the Body Responds to Stress

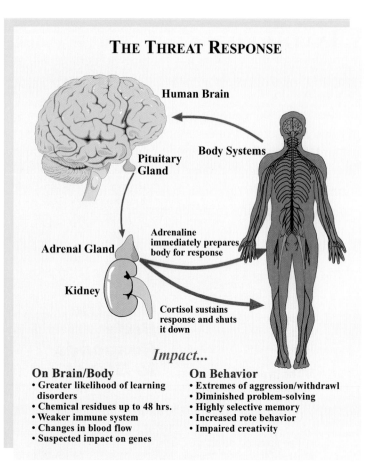

THE THREAT RESPONSE

Human Brain

Pituitary Gland

Body Systems

Adrenal Gland

Adrenaline immediately prepares body for response

Kidney

Cortisol sustains response and shuts it down

Impact...

On Brain/Body
- Greater likelihood of learning disorders
- Chemical residues up to 48 hrs.
- Weaker immune system
- Changes in blood flow
- Suspected impact on genes

On Behavior
- Extremes of aggression/withdrawl
- Diminished problem-solving
- Highly selective memory
- Increased rote behavior
- Impaired creativity

Reticular Activating System

This area of the brain acts as an orienting mechanism that helps us identify a particular direction for a response. When threatened, it initiates the cascade of chemical reactions that mobilize the mind and body for preservation.

Hippocampus

This crescent-shaped structure, located within the temporal lobes in the lower middle part of the brain, may be the most susceptible to acute or chronic distress. For example, some loss in size of the hippocampus has been noted in PTSD cases. Clearly, a typical stressor experienced in a normal day, however, does not constitute acute distress. Rather, it is 4 to 8 weeks or more of acute exposure that have been shown to ultimately suppress dendritic growth and neuron maintenance in the hippocampus region—specific to episodic and semantic memory. Adrenal steroids—released in response to stress—inhibit cell proliferation in the dentate gyrus during the early postnatal period and in adulthood. It is not clear whether the cell loss is permanent or a "reversible atrophy." Today scientists are convinced, however, that our brain can grow new cells, and enrichment seems to accelerate the process.

Caudate Nucleus and Putamen

Chronic psychosocial conflict decreases dopamine transporter binding sites in motor-related brain areas, resulting in a reduction in locomotor activity.

Genes

Mice lacking corticotropin-releasing hormone receptors exhibit more distress and anxious behaviors than do normal mice.

Cerebral Blood Flow

Adults with PTSD exhibit increased cerebral blood flow in anterior paralimbic regions and orbitofrontal and anterior temporal regions.

Frontal Lobes

Studies implicate dysfunction of the medial prefrontal cortex (subcallosal gyrus and anterior cingulate). Activation in these brain areas may be a result of a reactivation occurrence in PTSD sufferers. Under threat, there's a decrease in blood flow to the anterior dorsal area of the frontal lobes (higher, up front), which manages our executive function, short-term memory, planning, thinking, and creativity. In addition, there's an increase in blood flow to the anterior ventral frontal (lower, up front) areas, which are used for emotional processing. These changes increase the likelihood that the distressed student will be flooded with emotions, making him/her less able to resolve the problem at hand. In short, the greater the exposure to threat, the less blood flows to the areas of the brain needed for thinking and learning.

 # RECOGNIZABLE SYMPTOMS

A highly distressed or somewhat traumatized student will generally react in one of two ways. The brain responds to distress by hypersecretion of glucocorticoids. The net effect is a habituation and eventual desensitization to stress that we call numbness. The opposite reaction, hypervigilance, may also occur. Hypervigilant students are always on red alert for danger, scanning the environment for verbal or non-verbal cues of impending threat. A student who is severely distressed does not "snap out of it" quickly. Count on it to take some time.

COMMON STRESS DISORDER SYMPTOMS

▼ Boredom and listlessness
▼ Lack of energy
▼ Short-term memory loss
▼ Below average episodic (spatial) memory
▼ Inability to prioritize
▼ Careless work

▼ Below average social skills
▼ Frequent drug use—particularly marijuana and cocaine
▼ Loss of creativity
▼ Poor concentration
▼ Increased rote behavior—lack of creativity

The following symptom clusters are associated with Acute Stress Disorder and PTSD:

1. Recurring intrusive recollections of the traumatic event such as dreams and flashbacks.
2. Persistent avoidance of stimuli associated with the trauma or numbing of general responsiveness.
3. Persistent increased arousal characterized by hypervigilance, increased startle response, sleep difficulties, irritability, anxiety, and physiological hyperactivity. They may lose interest in things they used to enjoy and have trouble feeling affectionate. They may feel irritable, more aggressive than before, or even violent—all conditions that severely inhibit learning.

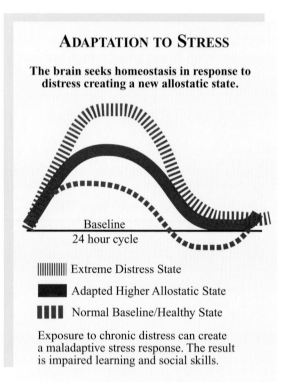

ADAPTATION TO STRESS

The brain seeks homeostasis in response to distress creating a new allostatic state.

Baseline
24 hour cycle

|||||||| Extreme Distress State

███ Adapted Higher Allostatic State

|||| Normal Baseline/Healthy State

Exposure to chronic distress can create a maladaptive stress response. The result is impaired learning and social skills.

The symptoms of Acute Distress Disorder and PTSD can range from mild to severe. Sufferers may become easily irritated or have violent outbursts. In severe cases they may have trouble working or socializing. In general, the symptoms seem to be worse if the event that triggered them was initiated by a person, such as a rape, as opposed to a disaster, such as a flood.

Unfortunately, ordinary classroom events can serve as reminders of the trauma and trigger flashbacks or intrusive images. Flashbacks can cause a temporary distortion of reality in sufferers that may last for a period of seconds, hours, or occasionally, days. A flashback, which consists of images, sounds, smells, and/or feelings, can be so real in the sufferer's mind that he/she actually relives the trauma each time the flashback occurs.

 **WHAT YOU CAN DO**

Chances are pretty good that a student dealing with threat or chronic distress will seem out of sorts. He/she will be coping, not thriving. You can make a difference by providing a positive learning environment with consistent daily routines and expectations. Role model good stress management skills and, when appropriate, incorporate into lesson plans such activities as deep breathing, stretching, visualization, goal-setting, good eating habits, problem-solving, and exercise. Distressed learners will likely need more of a boost to get them into the learning groove and keep them engaged. Some ways you can help reduce the student's stress include the following:

✓ **Give learners opportunities for personal control and decision making.**
✓ **Offer predictability through overviews, routines, rituals, and reviews.**
✓ **Help students find positive outlets for their frustration.**
✓ **Reinforce the belief that conditions can and will improve despite temporary setbacks.**
✓ **Role model good stress management and problem-solving skills.**

As an Educator

The strategies presented in this section represent generally sound teaching practices; thus, they'll benefit all of your students! However, when incorporated into a consistent classroom routine, they can have a powerful effect on distressed learners. Merely discovering that success at school is a realistic possibility can be a life-changing experience for the distressed learner. Many successful adults raised in troubled homes or faced with early life trauma attribute their achievements later in life to the support of a caring teacher who helped them cope with their stress and channel their energy productively.

Of course, these strategies don't need to be implemented all at once. Initiate one at a time if you wish. Soon they'll become a natural part of your daily classroom routine. It is important to make it reasonably easy for learners to experience success in your classroom. Be sure your expectations are realistic, clearly communicated, and consistently reinforced. When the student achieves a goal, validate their success. Once the powerful cycle of empowerment/motivation/achievement is set in motion, students learn they can channel their energy into either positive or negative directions. They come to understand that it is their own daily decisions that ultimately determine the course of their life.

Personalize Your Attention

When interacting with students, use their first name. Make sure your first and last interactions of the day are positive. Students tend to recall the first and last things you say. If they are greeted with a frown or complaint day after day, soon they'll associate school with drudgery and negativity.

Incorporate More Physical Activity

Start the day with a movement activity to get the blood flowing and regularly break up seatwork with physical activity throughout the day. Facilitate a stretching or deep breathing session, a group assignment, or a walk-and-talk time. Games, relays, experiments, or moving to music are other ways to get physical. Teach students the stress-management value of slow deep breathing and stretching, which increase oxygen to the brain and body. Also encourage emotional release and stress reduction through art, creative writing, drama, and music.

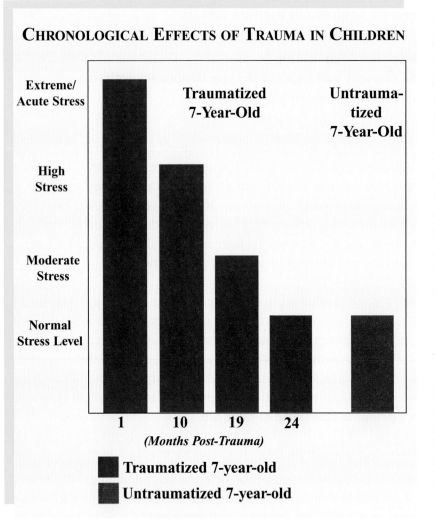

CHRONOLOGICAL EFFECTS OF TRAUMA IN CHILDREN

Extreme/Acute Stress · High Stress · Moderate Stress · Normal Stress Level

Traumatized 7-Year-Old — Untraumatized 7-Year-Old

1   10   19   24
(Months Post-Trauma)

■ Traumatized 7-year-old
■ Untraumatized 7-year-old

Get Connected

Give students ample opportunities to interact with each other. Take a few moments yourself to check in with students in a brief, personal way. Share something you enjoyed over the weekend—a new discovery, a funny story, or a personal learning experience. The relationship a teacher establishes with his/her students is an important factor in teaching and learning success. Journaling and peer discussions are also effective strategies for helping distressed learners identify and cope with their trauma/stress.

Establish Routines

A ritual is a dependable event (i.e., reciting The Pledge of Allegiance each morning). A routine is a string of rituals. All of us follow rituals and routines every day, either consciously or unconsciously, for example, when getting ready for work. Classroom rituals and routines help anchor students—a practice that is especially important for distressed learners. Provide regular overviews so students can anticipate the learning objectives for the day, week, month, and year. Make the rituals fun and meaningful. For example, you might incorporate a daily three-minute drawing and sharing session.

Incorporate Stress-Reduction Strategies

Teach students ways to regulate their own stress levels such as relaxation techniques, yoga, singing, artwork, "taking a breather," conflict resolution skills, managing self-talk, visualization, and physical exercise or movement.

Restore Motivation

Distressed students often suffer from lack of motivation as a result of feeling unempowered or overpowered by others. Offset this problem with the following five "brain-compatible" teaching principles:

1. Eliminate Threat: Avoid placing unrealistic demands on students such as giving assignments without the necessary resources and support to accomplish them. Do not make statements in a threatening tone such as, "Unless you do this.. you're going to have to..." Avoid embarrassing students in front of their peers, punishing them, putting them on the spot, or calling on them when they didn't volunteer. Honor students' answers, whether they're correct or not. Be sensitive to their feelings.

2. Encourage Goal-Setting: Encourage students to set daily, weekly, and long-term goals. Check in with them on a regular basis, provide feedback, and validate their progress. For example, ask students to share their goals with classmates by posting them as timelines or charts. "Public recognition" is a great motivator and strategy for reinforcing progress. Once a distressed learner sets a goal, do everything in your power to help him/her succeed.

3. Activate Emotions: Engage learners in creative projects that incorporate drawing, painting, music making, building, dancing, and performing. Engage learners with movement activities such as relays, games, stretching, Simon Says, walks, and energizers. Encourage a feeling of purpose through meaningful projects, such as service work, yearbooks, community competitions, journal-keeping, directories, and political activism.

4. Increase Feedback: Students are typically starved for feedback. The traditional primary mechanisms for feedback—test results and semester grades—are not sufficient in themselves to assist students in reaching coursework objectives. Feedback can be increased quite simply by increasing the means for providing it. It does not have to be given by the teacher every time. Peer collaboration and teamwork can play an important role in the feedback process. A basic guideline is to make sure students receive some form of feedback every half hour. Some ways you can increase feedback sources is to incorporate peer editing, self-recorded audiotapes, wall progress charts, checklists, student check-ins and reviews, friendly competitions, group process and observation, cross-age tutoring, computer-assisted instruction, and peer and self-reflection opportunities. Tie your feedback to the student's personal goals, being sure to offset constructive criticism with positive reinforcement of progress.

5. Provide a Positive Learning Climate: Provide ample acknowledgment of individual and group accomplishments and efforts. Increase the number and types of classroom celebrations and team activities. Take notice of birthdays, special events, and cultural or community activities. Keep up with current events and encourage learners to do the same. Incorporate "real-life" experiences into the curriculum as frequently as you can. Little rituals, such as celebrating the completion of a new unit with a group success chant, can go a long way towards warming classroom climate and reinforcing positive accomplishments.

AS A PARENT

If you suspect your child is suffering from Acute Stress Disorder or PTSD, take immediate steps toward diagnosis and treatment. Regardless of age, this is a serious and debilitating problem, and treatment should not be delayed. Seek advice from a qualified medical professional and psychologist. Treatment options include drug therapy, psychotherapy, and group therapy. A program of behavioral modification is sometimes successful without additional intervention.

Gather Information

Try to determine the source of the chronic stress/threat and eliminate it. If the stress is related to family dynamics, consider family therapy and/or positive parenting classes. If the stress is related to the child's school environment, make an appointment with the teacher and/or administrators to assess the problem. It may be necessary to change teachers or schools if the problem is not resolved.

Consider Therapy

✓ **Cognitive-Behavioral Therapy**

This therapy modality emphasizes self-talk awareness and coping skills using various tools such as breath retraining and biofeedback. Objectives of therapy might include, for example, learning to reframe negative thinking patterns ("cognitive restructuring"), managing anger, preparing for stress reactions ("stress inoculation"), handling future trauma symptoms, coping with urges to use alcohol or drugs ("relapse prevention"), and communicating and relating effectively with people (social skills and/or intimacy patterns).

✓ **Group Therapy**

The group setting is often effective as it provides survivors with support and feedback from other survivors of similar trauma. Sharing traumatic experiences in a safe, cohesive, and empathetic environment or "telling one's story" (the "trauma narrative") helps sufferers face and move through the grief, anxiety, and guilt that is often associated with intense distress and trauma. Group therapy has facilitated the recovery of many survivors who are then able to go on with their lives, rather than sinking into a chasm of unspoken despair and helplessness.

✓ **Brief Psychodynamic Psychotherapy**

This therapy modality focuses on the emotional conflicts at the root of the trauma or distress. The therapist helps the patient identify current life situations that set off traumatic memories and worsen PTSD symptoms.

✓ **Exposure Therapy**

This modality helps patients confront a past trauma by repeatedly imagining it in great detail. Sometimes this is initiated in the therapist's office or, in some instances, requires going to the place(s) where the trauma occurred. This purposeful recurrence is intended to help the patient face and gain control of the fear and distress that is associated with the root trauma. In some cases, trauma memories or reminders can be confronted all at once ("flooding"), while in other cases, a gradual approach is necessary.

✓ **Eye Movement Desensitization Reprocessing (EMDR)**

EMDR is a relatively new, short-term approach to therapy that is sometimes effective in just a single one-hour session. The therapist suggests certain images while guiding the client through a series of structured eye movements.

Consider Medication

Drug therapy is sometimes used to reduce the anxiety, depression, emotional numbness, and insomnia often associated with PTSD or trauma memories. The antidepressant Zoloft (a selective serotonin reuptake inhibitor or SSRI) was the first government-approved treatment for relieving the nightmares and emotional problems caused by PTSD. Medications are useful for symptom relief, thereby making it possible for patients to participate in group, psychodynamic, cognitive-behavioral, or other forms of psychotherapy.

Multiple therapeutic approaches are often used in conjunction with each other; however, when the therapy is too diverse or intense, the client can become overwhelmed and confused—a counterproductive result.

MEMORY JOGGER

 Remember this face? This is "Mary," one of the learners introduced in the pretest at the front of the book. She's also the student who fits the profile for chronic threat and distress. Like the others, Mary is unique—she exhibits a pattern of symptoms that are associated with a specific disorder. However, some of these symptoms can be observed in other conditions as well. This is why you want to look for *patterns* rather than *isolated behaviors*. To help you remember what's important in assessing a stress disorder, take a moment, relax, and focus on the photo, the symptoms, and the key points of this chapter.

Symptoms

- Seems to be edgy and on alert
- Trance-like state is common; doesn't "snap out of it" quickly
- Appears bored and disconnected
- Short-term memory loss and inability to prioritize

- Makes careless errors in her work
- Decreased social contact
- Doesn't remember "where" questions
- Loss of creativity and poor concentration
- Seems to be sick more often than peers

SUPPLEMENTAL RESOURCES

Books

Why Zebras Don't Get Ulcers, by Robert Sapolsky
EMDR: The Breakthrough Therapy, by Francine Shapiro
Motivation and Learning, by Rogers, Ludington, and Graham
Active Learning: 101 Strategies, by Mel Silberman

Websites

www.cyberpsych.org *(Anxiety Disorders Association of America)*

Organizations

National Anxiety Foundation
3135 Custer Drive
Lexington, KY 40517

American Psychiatric Association
1400 K Street, N.W.
Washington, DC 20005
202-682-6000
www.psych.org

Anxiety Disorders Association of America, Inc.
11900 Parklawn Drive, Suite 100
Rockville, MD 20852-2624
301-231-9350
www.adaa.org

International Society for Traumatic Stress
Studies
60 Revere Drive, Suite 500
Northbrook, IL 60062
847-480-9028
www.istss.org

National Center for PTSD
VA Medical Center (116D)
White River Junction, VT 05009
802-296-5132
www.dartmouth.edu/dms/ptsd

National Institute of Mental Health Public
Inquiries
6001 Executive Blvd., Room 8184 MSC 9663
Bethesda, MD 20892-9663
301-443-4513
FACTS ON DEMAND: 301-443-5158
www.nimh.nih.gov

10

The Troubled Learner: Depression

 ## OVERVIEW

Depression is an intense, pervasive, and serious mood disorder that attacks both the mind and body. This highly disruptive condition typically impairs academic performance, job performance, family life, and can sometimes lead to suicide. The following four categories of depression are commonly used to diagnose the severity of the condition.

Major Depressive Disorder is the most common form of depression and is characterized by at least five major symptoms, including melancholy, loss of energy, impaired concentration, insomnia, hypersomnia, anxiety, and diminished libido. Characterized by either single or recurrent episodes, this form of depression can reach mild, moderate, or severe levels, and can hinder occupational, social, and interpersonal relationships. Sufferers who experience recurrent episodes are more likely to have suicidal thoughts than those who experience a single episode.

Dysthymic Disorder is a milder form of depression that lasts a minimum of two years. It is the second most common type of depression, but because sufferers tend to accept its relatively mild symptoms as "normal," it often goes overlooked, undiagnosed, and untreated. Typically, dysthymia begins at age 7 or 8 and can last a lifetime. Severity increases with recurrent episodes.

Bipolar Disorder (formerly known as Manic-Depressive Disorder) is a severe and chronic "roller-coaster" illness characterized by both extreme highs and lows. The symptoms of Bipolar Disorder are similar to those of major depression with certain variations such as mania and intense mood swings. Bipolar depression is just as crippling as major depression, even during euphoric phases. More than 80 percent of bipolar sufferers will eventually recover if early intervention takes place. Some believe that the longer bipolar depression goes untreated, the more damage is done to the brain. The disorder has a strong genetic link.

Seasonal Affective Disorder is a form of depression that follows seasonal rhythms with symptoms occurring in the winter months and diminishing in spring and summer. Some researchers believe that this disorder may be a mild version of bipolar depression. Individuals most depressed in the winter are among the most elated in the summer

 # IMPACT

In some cases, a clinical diagnosis of depression is possible in children by age 5 or 6. Typically, major depressive episodes last 9 to 12 months. More than 80 percent of depressives improve with treatment by the end of year one. Even if untreated, the symptoms may disappear temporarily, but the risk remains substantial for other adverse behaviors (i.e., drug abuse, suicide, sleep disorders). Anxiety is a common symptom of depression, often becoming so severe that sufferers stay in bed to cope with the symptom. This severe level of anxiety is also observed in individuals suffering from an actual anxiety disorder. Anxiety, as well as many other overlapping conditions, often occur in conjunction with depression.

 # DEMOGRAPHICS

The American Academy of Pediatrics (AAP) estimates that 5 percent of American children are depressed. More than 500,000 children in America are currently taking antidepressants, and the National Institute of Mental Health estimates that 10 percent of children suffer from a serious emotional disturbance. Among adolescents, the AAP estimates that as many as one in eight experience depression, and 10 percent of teens with major depression will commit suicide. Suicide rates among children and teens tripled between 1962 and 1995. A child who experiences even one episode of depression is twice as likely to be depressed in adulthood. Recurrent episodes of depression in adulthood are more likely if the initial onset occurred during adolescence.

Currently, one in six Americans will suffer from major depression at some point during their lifetime. About 13 to 20 percent of the population exhibit some depressive symptoms at any given time. Approximately 18 million Americans currently experience depression, one million of whom experience a severe, treatment-resistant form of the illness.

Prior to puberty, depression rates are equal among girls and boys; however, the number increases disproportionately for women later. Women are more prone to both depression and panic attacks; twice as many women, in fact, experience depression. However, more men than women suffer from drug and alcohol abuse. And while everybody, including children, can develop the illness, individuals with less education and lower income levels are more vulnerable to it.

COMMENTARY

Depression is serious and should be treated immediately. However, identification and treatment can be difficult since this complex disorder is so often accompanied by overlapping conditions. Some commonly observed comorbid conditions are alcohol or drug abuse, anxiety disorders, social phobias, and Obsessive-Compulsive Disorder. Thirty to fifty percent of depressives experience anxiety disorders; 10 to 30 percent experience conduct disorders; 20 to 30 percent experience substance abuse; and 50 to 60 percent experience personality disorders. Repeated episodes of major depression can lead to suicidal thoughts if left untreated.

Depression constitutes a high level of challenge to the classroom teacher. You can contribute to this learner's success, but you will need support from others—notably from parents and mental-health professionals.

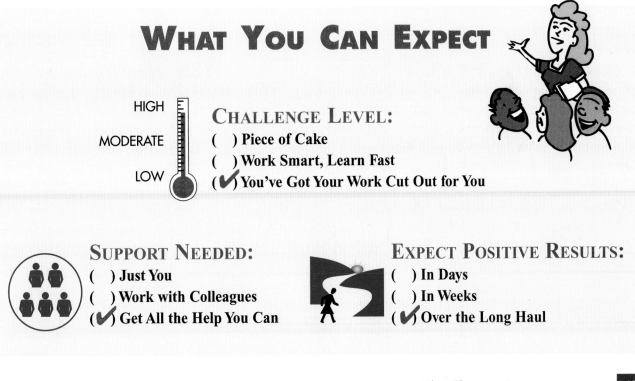

WHAT YOU CAN EXPECT

HIGH
MODERATE
LOW

CHALLENGE LEVEL:
( ) Piece of Cake
( ) Work Smart, Learn Fast
(✔) You've Got Your Work Cut Out for You

SUPPORT NEEDED:
( ) Just You
( ) Work with Colleagues
(✔) Get All the Help You Can

EXPECT POSITIVE RESULTS:
( ) In Days
( ) In Weeks
(✔) Over the Long Haul

❓ LIKELY CAUSES

While antidepressant drugs may alleviate some symptoms, they don't treat the cause. The following sections describe some of the more common explanations for depression.

Chemical Dysregulation

Imbalances in neurotransmitter levels in the brain impact the way an individual responds to daily events. For example, a low level of serotonin is the most common implication for the cause of depression. The medications prescribed for depression, Serotonin Selective Reuptake Inhibitors (SSRIs), increase levels of serotonin, resulting in the effective treatment of the majority of depressed patients who take these medications.

Additional evidence of the serotonin link includes reduced levels of serotonin by-products found in the cerebrospinal fluid of depressed and suicidal patients. Moreover, one of the most common receptors for serotonin starts to vanish from the human brain at the age of 20 and continues to decline into old age at a rate of about 15 percent every decade. This finding, presented at the 29th annual meeting of The Society for Neuroscience in Miami, could explain why depression is most commonly diagnosed in middle age and hardest to treat in the elderly.

Gender

In a survey of 1,393 people from Toronto, researchers at the organization called Social Support Goes Both Ways found a strong association between emotional reliance and depression. Results suggested that women were significantly more likely to be emotionally reliant than men, independent of other factors like social status, marital status, education, income, and job prestige. In addition, women appeared more deeply impacted by their emotional reliance than men, and emotionally reliant men were less likely to be depressed than emotionally reliant women participating in the study.

Cytokines (Inflammatory Mediators)

Major depression is associated with the dysfunction of inflammatory mediators called cytokines. Several lines of evidence indicate that brain cytokines, principally interleukin-1beta (IL-1beta) and IL-1 receptor antagonist, may play a role in the biology of major depression, and they might additionally affect the pathophysiology, somatic consequences, and treatment effectiveness of depression.

Distress

Whether chronic or acute, distress increases the likelihood of depression. Extreme stress may impair the brain's ability to deal with change, further increasing the risk of depression. Ironically, children who are sheltered from life's stressful challenges are also at higher risk for depression. Children need moderately stressful experiences to develop their resiliency—a personal strength that will help them avert depression later in life.

Seasonal Darkness

Current research indicates that a seasonal reduction of sunlight can trigger a biochemical reaction in some individuals that may cause loss of energy, decreased activity, increased sadness, and excessive eating and sleeping. The condition is called Seasonal Affect Disorder.

UNDER-ACTIVITY AND HYPERACTIVITY IN THE BRAINS OF DEPRESSIVES

The brains of depressives are underactive in the prefrontal cortex

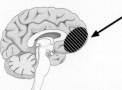

Paradoxically, the brains of depressives are hyperactive in (1) the cingulate gyrus and (2) the lateral area of the parietal and temporal lobes

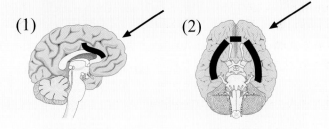

Smoking

Sufferers of major depression are more likely to smoke and to experience difficulty trying to quit. When such individuals do manage to quit, they are at increased risk of experiencing mild to severe states of depression, including full-blown major depression.

Brain Cell Deficiency

Recent studies on depression have implicated a small brain area located behind the bridge of the nose called the subgenual prefrontal cortex. In depressives, this area has been found to contain an average of 39 to 48 percent less brain tissue. In addition, it was found to be 8 percent less active in depressed individuals compared to unaffected individuals. It also was found to contain 41 percent fewer glial cells.

Malnutrition

Psychological symptoms are often associated with a deficiency in several vitamins/minerals, such as a folate deficiency in the elderly. In four double-blind studies, an improvement in thiamin balance was associated with improved mood. Iron-deficiency, a particularly common condition in women, is also associated with apathy, depression, and rapid fatigue during exercise.

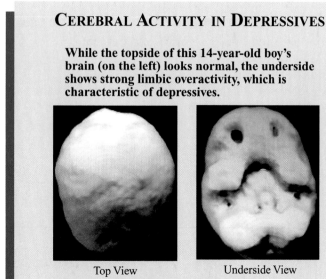

CEREBRAL ACTIVITY IN DEPRESSIVES

While the topside of this 14-year-old boy's brain (on the left) looks normal, the underside shows strong limbic overactivity, which is characteristic of depressives.

Top View   Underside View

Source: *Images into Human Behavior: A Brain SPECT Atlas*,
Daniel G. Amen, MD, 2000

Heredity

Depression and Bipolar Disorder frequently run in families. Close blood relatives of depressives are more likely to suffer from the condition than are individuals without a depressed family member.

Studies of identical (genetically indistinguishable) and fraternal twins support an inherited component. The finding of manic-depression in both members of a pair of identical twins is much higher than in fraternal twins. For example, if an *identical* twin suffers from manic depression, the other twin has a 50 percent chance of developing it, too; whereas, in *fraternal* twins the likelihood decreases to 10 percent. Other siblings of depressed individuals also run a 10 percent risk of developing the disorder.

 # BRAIN AREAS LIKELY INVOLVED

Basal Ganglia

Reports suggest that severe depression occurs 40 percent more often among individuals with lesions in the basal ganglia—an area containing an abundance of neurotransmitters and receptors.

Cingulate Gyrus

This brain area, located behind the frontal lobes, is often implicated in depression. It is one of the areas removed in a frontal lobotomy—the controversial surgery that used to be commonly performed in severe cases of depression.

Limbic Area

This deep frontal midbrain area is typically overactive in depressives. It includes the hypothalamus, thalamus, and olfactory areas, which are involved in bonding, smell, and sexuality. In addition, it includes the amygdala and hippocampus, two structures responsible for memory, emotion, and perception.

Frontal Lobes

The subgenual prefrontal cortex, a small area behind the bridge of the nose, has been shown to be less active and to contain less brain tissue in depressed individuals.

RECOGNIZABLE SYMPTOMS

One challenge in recognizing depression is that human beings are, by nature, mood variable. We're happy; we're sad; we're anxious; we're calm. Considering the number of daily factors capable of influencing mood, such as hunger, fatigue, or stress, it's easy to understand how depression could be mistaken for moodiness. But the symptoms of depression, unlike the symptoms of a temporary mood swing, are chronic and debilitating. They negatively impact an individual's ability to function at work, school, and in relationships. Depressed individuals often feel:

▼ **Numb**
▼ **Apathetic**
▼ **Anxious**
▼ **Disconnected**
▼ **Uncaring**

Symptoms of Major Depression

- Persistent sadness and withdrawal
- Inability to experience pleasure
- "I'm stupid" or "I'm worthless"
- Loss of interest in favorite things
- "I wish I could just disappear"
- Fatigue, indecision, loss of energy
- Excessive guilt or sadness
- Changes in sleep habits or weight
- New multiple symptoms over time

5% of children age 5-18 are "significantly depressed."
500,000+ children are taking antidepressants.
1 of 10 kids w/ major depression will commit suicide.
80% of runaways suffer from depression.

The depressed patient may find it difficult to reveal or discuss these subjective emotional states—a problem that can make diagnosis even more challenging. But the outward signs and symptoms indicating depression are numerous and persistent. Common signs to look for include the following:

▼ **Decreased or increased appetite leading to weight change**
▼ **Insomnia or hypersomnia**
▼ **Feelings of worthlessness and guilt**
▼ **Inability to think clearly or concentrate effectively**
▼ **Indecisiveness**
▼ **Persistent sad, anxious, or empty moods**
▼ **Feelings of hopelessness or pessimism**
▼ **Loss of interest or pleasure in ordinary activities**
▼ **Decreased energy and fatigue**
▼ **Restlessness or irritability**
▼ **Unexplained aches and pains**
▼ **Thoughts of death or suicide**
▼ **Anxiety**
▼ **Loss of friends**
▼ **Diminished academic performance (However, very bright and perfection-oriented children are often able to maintain good grades in spite of their depression.)**

 # WHAT YOU CAN DO

If untreated, depression may lead to the development of other serious problems. For example, depressed students are more prone to substance abuse, anxiety, delusions, and, the most dire consequence, suicide. These individuals are also more likely to develop speech disorders and learning problems. Don't delay in seeking immediate help. At the very least consult with the depressed student's parents and with your school psychologist. Once you have done your part to encourage therapeutic intervention, you can help the depressed student in the classroom by providing a positive environment, consistency, and extra emotional support.

As an Educator

Seek Support

Encourage a response team approach. Any efforts or steps being taken by parents, teachers, administrators, counselors, physicians, or the student him/herself should be communicated to the response team. Make sure everyone's working together towards the same goals and objectives, and that the parties most emotionally involved (i.e., student, parents, teachers) feel supported by the team.

Incorporate Physical Activity

Movement and exercise can increase the production of the "feel-good" neurotransmitters that are beneficial in coping with the negative emotions of depression. Incorporate walks, relays, field trips, stretching, aerobics, and Brain Gym activities into your curriculum.

Teach Coping Skills

Teach students to think positively about themselves and their problems as a way to generate new options for their lives. Help them recognize that many possible interpretations of any event exist and that they can choose the most empowering one. Illustrate for them the cycle of thinking and feeling that leads to bad outcomes (See illustration in Chapter 2, page 25.)

As a Parent

Since depressed adolescents are especially vulnerable to drugs and suicide, your positive reaction to their condition is an essential lifeline. Foster a sense that they have some control over their lives, that what they do is different from who they are, and that they are loved despite their condition.

Although in the most severe and chronic cases the patient may require hospitalization, different types of depression require a variety of approaches. The key is to obtain an accurate diagnosis quickly and then experiment with the various treatments until the symptoms are relieved. Depression rarely improves without intervention. It is a chronic and invasive disorder that without treatment can threaten academic success social relationships. Take depression seriously.

Although 80 percent of depressed patients recover over a two-year period, they do not necessarily achieve a complete cure. Rather, their depression becomes dormant. For how long? No one knows, but the patient's history of recurrent depressive episodes may be the best indicator. Many psychiatrists support the theory that depression is never cured, only treated. They believe that, like cancer, it goes into remission but may never fully leave the body and mind. Expect to use medication for at least 12 months, even if the symptoms are alleviated, and be aware that symptoms could return in a week without medication!

Teach Effective Life Skills

Children, if old enough, can be retrained to think about themselves and their problems more optimistically. Show them how to generate new options and solutions for their lives. And consider coupling your efforts at home with short-term, goal-oriented therapy to further engender a more positive view of their life.

Obtain Psychotherapeutic Counseling

Professional counseling can help the depressed individual develop new ways of thinking, new ways of dealing with others, and new ways of resolving conflicts. Studies suggest that cognitive and interpersonal therapy provide effective treatment for mild to moderate depression. To a lesser degree, psychoanalytical and behavioral therapies have also been shown to be effective.

Although psychotherapy can be effective in treating mild to moderate depression, its effectiveness in treating hospitalized patients and those with severe depression has not been proven. Nor has psychotherapy been shown to prevent recurrent depressive episodes. In a study of hospitalized patients with recurrent depression (responsive to a combination of the antidepressant Imipramine and interpersonal psychotherapy), maintenance psychotherapy alone helped prevent new episodes, but was not as effective as maintenance therapy combined with Imipramine.

Seek the Advice of a Physician/Psychiatrist

In a survey of physicians, only 8 percent of pediatricians said they had training in dealing with childhood depression. However, 72 percent said that they had prescribed Serotonin Selective Reuptake Inhibitors for children, and 40 percent said they did so in combination with other drugs. If you feel your child's primary physician is not able to effectively treat the problem, seek the advice of a psychiatrist who specializes in children's mental disorders.

Consider Medication

Studies on the effects of antidepressants in children are limited. However, in one study, 50 percent of the children taking antidepressants improved compared to 30 percent of the children taking a sugar pill (placebo).

In cases of moderate to severe depression, stronger medication may be required to effectively treat the disorder. Typically, only half of all patients get relief with their first medication, a problem partly due to the many variables in human brain chemistry. However, if one drug does not work initially, other brands should be tried. Twenty-two different antidepressants from eight different mechanistically-defined classes of antidepressants are available. While all prescriptive antidepressants have side effects, some of the newer drugs have fewer.

Women, more often than men, are unresponsive to antidepressants. Of the women who take antidepressants, 20 percent do not show improvement from depressive symptoms. Moreover, an individual who's been depressed for 20 or more years is more likely to be unresponsive to medication. His or her brain may have changed too dramatically to be impacted by antidepressant medications.

Bipolar depression is the most difficult to treat. While Lithium can be used to treat *unipolar* depression, *bipolar* depression is tricky and does not always respond to this drug. However, in some bipolar cases, Lithium will elicit a marked improvement, but is most effective in patients who've had three or fewer bipolar episodes. In 30 percent of bipolar patients, Lithium diminishes the mania but doesn't treat the depression. These individuals may need a more common antidepressant like Prozac or anticonvulsant like Tegretol. Further research needs to be conducted to determine which medications are most effective for treating depression in all its forms.

Provide Nutritional Supplements

Give your child a high-quality multi-vitamin and mineral supplement on a daily basis. Supplements are most effective when taken twice per day. In addition, children with mild to moderate depression may benefit from over-the-counter approaches that are less invasive than prescription drugs. Listed below are some of the most popular nutritional supplements for this purpose:

▼ **St. John's Wort** (250mg X2/day)
▼ **L-Tyrosine** (750mg/day)
▼ **5-HTP** (Tryptophan) 1500mg/day
▼ **DLPA** (DL-phenylalanine) 200mg/day
▼ **SAM-E** (S-adenosyl-methionine) 100-200mg/day

The first three supplements listed on the previous page impact neurotransmitter levels with *little to no* reported side effects. Patients who have been unsuccessful with prescription medications often turn to these common healthfood store products. Experiment with dosages to find the right amount. Supplements typically take at least 10 days before the regulatory mechanisms in the brain rebalance, and some products aren't fully effective for up to a month.

 # MEMORY JOGGER

Remember this face? This is "Michele," one of the learners introduced in the pre-test at the front of the book. She's also the student who fits the profile for depression. Like the others, Michele is unique—she exhibits a pattern of symptoms that are associated with a specific disorder. However, some of these symptoms can be observed in other conditions as well. This is why you want to look for *patterns* rather than *isolated behaviors*. To help you remember what's important in assessing depression, take a moment, relax, and focus on the photo, the symptoms, and the key points of this chapter.

Symptoms

- Decrease in energy
- Change in appetite and subsequent weight
- Feelings of worthlessness and guilt
- Inability to think clearly or concentrate; indecisiveness
- Thoughts of death, suicidal imaginings
- Persistent sad, anxious, or empty mood

- Feelings of hopelessness; pessimism
- Loss of interest or pleasure in ordinary activities or hobbies
- Restlessness, irritability, unexplained aches and pains
- Unusual loss of friends, reduction in academic performance

SUPPLEMENTAL RESOURCES

Books

The Bipolar Child, by Janice Papolos
Major Depression: The Forgotten Illness, by Paul A. Kettl, MD
The Life of a Bipolar Child, by Trudy Carlson
Darkness Visible, by William Styron
Body Blues, by Laura Weeldreyer
Ups and Downs: How to Beat the Blues, by Susan Klebanoff
How to Cope with Depression, by Raymond DePaulo
Teen Depression, by Lisa Wolf
The Unquiet Mind, by Kay Redfield Jamison
Coping with Teen Suicide, by James Murphy

Websites

www.unisci.com

Organizations

Dr. Ivan's Depression Central
Information on all types of depressive disorders and the most effective treatments for major depression, manic depression, cyclothymia, dysthymia, and other mood disorders. www.psycom.net

Mental Health InfoSource
A collection of resources providing information on disorders such as substance abuse, anxiety, depression, eating disorders, schizophrenia, and sexual dysfunction. Includes information on drug development and manufacturers, and offers an opportunity to pose questions to medical experts on mental health issues. www.mhsource.com

Jerome Marmorstein
Chairman of the Environmental Health Committee of the California Medical Association and Assistant Clinical Professor of Medicine, USC College of Medicine, Los Angeles, California.

Neural Development Group
The Advanced BioScience Laboratories/Basic Research Program of the National Cancer Institute/Frederick Cancer Research and Development Center, Frederick, Maryland.

New Health Center
An automated catalogue of numerous mailing lists relevant to specific complaints and other aspects of medicine and health care, with descriptions and subscription details. new.health-center.com

IN CLOSING

11

In Closing

This book is *not* about *all* learners who fall through the cracks, only the most common. Even if *Different Brains, Different Learners* were three times as long, it would still be difficult to explore each condition that impacts students today. Every kind of learner passes through our classroom doors, and every one of them deserves to succeed. As we enter this twenty-first century, we are clearly faced with a huge challenge.

Perhaps the greatest concern among educators at the moment is the disproportionate class time used to produce higher test scores—a present-day dilemma that can mean less attention to individualized instruction, life skills, the arts, and for reaching troubled learners. But there is a deeper question we should be asking: What will prepare learners most for life success—higher test scores or a well-rounded education? What business are we in—the information business or the people business? I say, we're in the *people* business!

Can we do both? Can we groom a child for life success *and* achieve higher test scores? YES! But our priority must be clear. If we focus *first* on people, we can trust that tests scores will ultimately improve. But if we focus *first* on testing, we can expect that learners will undoubtedly suffer—especially the ones who need us most.

My hope in writing *Different Brains, Different Learners* is that you'll become better equipped to successfully identify and address the learning impairments that are so common today, yet often neglected in teacher-education programs. It is easy to feel overwhelmed when you think of implementing all the strategies in this book. But relax and take one step at a time. Ultimately you will become a much more efficient, effective, and rewarded teacher of diverse learners.

With your increased awareness you'll spend less time and energy with problems you can't control; you'll minimize disruptions to the rest of the class; you'll learn how to accommodate the various disorders; and you'll understand when it is important to refer the student out for expert consultation. All of us already work hard, so working harder is not the answer: We have to work smarter! Remember, you make a difference: You change lives! Go on and do what you do best; and most importantly, enjoy the challenge!

Post-Test:
You'll Recognize These Learners Now!

LEARNER #1 "ASHLEY"

Symptoms

◆ Loses her temper often
◆ Argues with adults; defies authority and rejects adults' requests or rules; complies about 10 to 20 percent of the time
◆ Deliberately annoys others and is easily annoyed herself
◆ Blames others for her own mistakes or misbehavior
◆ Angry and resentful; vindictive for no apparent reason
◆ Swears and uses obscene language

Ashley is eight years old and smart. She's managed to get just about everyone in class mad at her. What's most likely going on? Answer:_____

LEARNER #2 "BRENT"

Symptoms

◆ Inattentive to others
◆ Easily distracted
◆ Engages in a lot of head turning to hear better
◆ Retrieval problems ("Um ....I forget the word")
◆ Difficulty following oral directions
◆ Omits word endings
◆ Speaks words out of order
◆ Mistaken words—says "starvation army" instead of Salvation Army or "fum" instead of thumb

This pattern began early, before he entered school. He's in the third grade, doing poorly, and he has not been tested. What's most likely going on? Answer:_____

LEARNER #3 "MICHELE"

Symptoms

◆ Decrease in energy
◆ Change in appetite and subsequent weight
◆ Feelings of worthlessness and guilt
◆ Inability to think clearly or concentrate; indecisiveness
◆ Thoughts of death, suicidal imaginings
◆ Persistent sad, anxious, or empty mood
◆ Feelings of hopelessness; pessimism
◆ Loss of interest or pleasure in ordinary activities or hobbies
◆ Restlessness, irritability, unexplained aches and pains
◆ Unusual loss of friends, reduction in academic performance

Michele is a fourth-grader who did well last year. This year her mother is being treated for cancer. What's most likely going on? Answer:_____

LEARNER #4 "JASON"

Symptoms

◆ Rarely finishes his work
◆ Calls out answers in class; never waits his turn
◆ Easily and consistently distracted
◆ Exhibits weak follow-through and preparation for future events
◆ Wants everything right away; no patience
◆ Personal areas (desk) are a mess
◆ Doesn't seem able to reflect on the past to learn from it
◆ Doesn't sit still; always on the go
◆ Can't hold several thoughts at a time
◆ Hindsight or foresight rarely evident

Jason is a second-grade student with plenty of enthusiasm. He gets average grades. What's most likely going on? Answer:_____

LEARNER #5 "LEE"

Symptoms

◆ Has trouble with sequencing, prioritizing, and completing tasks
◆ Takes spoken or written language literally
◆ Has difficulty following oral directions and remembering them
◆ Inability to rhyme by age four
◆ Confuses left and right, over and under, before and after, and other directionality words and concepts
◆ Lack of dominant handedness; switches hands between or even during tasks
◆ Unable to correctly complete phonemic awareness tasks
◆ Has difficulty learning the names and sounds of letters and writing them in alphabetical order

Lee, a seventh-grader, likes to read but struggles to maintain average grades. He rarely completes his assignments. What's most likely going on? Answer:_____

LEARNER #6 "JOSHUA"

Symptoms

◆ Inappropriate emotional outbursts with random acts of destruction
◆ Consistently hurtful towards peers—swatting, hitting, and verbal intimidation
◆ Refuses to follow directions directly; consistently challenges authority
◆ Loud and aggressive communication patterns, often taunting the teacher and using vulgar language
◆ Unwilling to participate with others in normal social activities
◆ Is prone to lie

This pattern began in first grade and has continued into high school.
What's most likely going on? Answer:_____

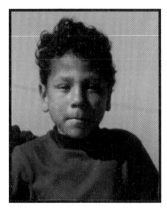

LEARNER #7 "MIGUEL"

Symptoms

◆ Difficulty structuring work time

◆ Impaired rates of learning and poor memory

◆ Has trouble generalizing behaviors and information

◆ Sometimes exhibits impulsive behavior

◆ Easily distracted and frequently exhibits reduced attention span

◆ Displays a sense of fearlessness and is unresponsive to verbal cautions

◆ Displays poor social judgment

◆ Has trouble internalizing modeled behaviors

◆ Language *production* is higher than *comprehension*

◆ Overall poor problem-solving strategies

◆ May have unusual facial features

Miguel has had these problems for years. In spite of this, he has been passed from one teacher to the next. What's most likely going on? Answer:_____

LEARNER #8 "COURTNEY"

Symptoms

◆ Displays a high level of apathy, listlessness, or lack of inertia

◆ Passive and unresponsive in spite of shocking or surprising events

◆ Does not initiate new activities or learning

◆ Does not feel in control of her environment; likely to say, "What's the point?" "Why bother?" "Who cares" or "So what?"

◆ Lack of hostility even when hostility is warranted

◆ Increased sarcasm

Courtney is twenty-one. She attends adult school because, if she doesn't, she will be kicked out of her house. The above symptoms have continued for about three to four months. Her teacher cannot quite nail down what's wrong. What's most likely going on? Answer:_____

LEARNER #9 "JEFFREY"

Symptoms

◆ Extreme fidgeting; stands instead of sits; walks instead of stands; and runs instead of walks
◆ Irritability and emotional immaturity
◆ Ignores routines and rules
◆ Exhibits continual action; does not use caution
◆ Constant tactile manipulation
◆ Often taps, touches, or pushes others

Jeffrey has exhibited this behavior pattern from a very early age. He seems to be on high power, while everyone else is operating at normal speed. What's most likely going on?

Answer:_____

LEARNER #10 "MARY"

Symptoms

◆ Seems to be edgy and on alert
◆ Trance-like state is common; doesn't "snap out of it" quickly
◆ Appears bored and disconnected
◆ Short-term memory loss and inability to prioritize
◆ Makes careless errors in her work
◆ Decreased social contact
◆ Doesn't remember "where" questions
◆ Loss of creativity and poor concentration
◆ Seems to be sick more often than peers

Mary, a high-school student, is struggling when, just a few years prior, she seemed so enthusiastic. Now it seems she is in a trance all the time. What's most likely going on?

Answer:_____

CONGRATULATIONS!

Bibliography

Amen, Daniel. 1998. *Change Your Brain, Change Your Life*. New York, NY: Times Books/Random House.

_____ 1997. *Images into the Mind: A Radical New Look at Understanding and Changing Behavior*. Fairfield, CA: MindWorks Press.

Ayd, Frank, J., Jr. 1995. *Lexicon of Psychiatry, Neurology, and the Neurosciences*. Baltimore, Maryland: Williams & Wilkins/A Waverly Company.

Ayres, Jean. 1973. *Sensory Integration and Learning Disorders*. Los Angeles, CA: Western Psychological Services.

Barkley, Russell. 1995. *Taking Charge of ADHD: The Complete Authoritative Guide for Parents*. New York, NY: The Guilford Press.

Barondes, Samuel. 1993. *Molecules and Mental Illness*. New York, NY: Scientific American Library.

Bennett, E. Gerald & Donna Woolf. 1991. *Substance Abuse: Pharmacologic, Developmental and Clinical Perspectives*. Albany, NY: Delmar Publishers, Inc.

Berg, Bruce (Ed). *Principles of Child Neurology*. San Francisco, CA: McGraw-Hill.

Byrne, John (Ed.). 1998. *Learning & Memory*. March/April, Volume 4 (6). Plainview, NY: Cold Spring Harbor Laboratory Press.

Carter, Rita. 1998. *Mapping the Mind*. Berkeley, CA: University of California Press.

Chipps, Esther; Norma Clanin; & Victor Campbell. 1992. *Neurologic Disorders*. St. Louis, Missouri: Mosby Year Book.

Claude-Pierre, Peggy. 1997. *The Secret Language of Eating Disorders*. New York, NY: Random House.

Donway, Walter (Ed.). 2000. *Cerebrum: The Dana Forum on Brain Science*. Winter, Vol. 2 (1). New York, NY: The Dana Press.

_____ 1999. *Cerebrum: The Dana Forum on Brain Science*. Spring, Vol. 1 (1). New York, NY: The Dana Press.

_____ 1999. *Cerebrum: The Dana Forum on Brain Science*. Fall, Vol. 1 (2). New York, NY: The Dana Press.

_____ 1998. *Cerebrum: The Dana Forum on Brain Science*. New York, NY: The Dana Press.

Feinberg, Todd & Martha Farah. 1997. *Behavioral Neurology and Neuropsychology*. San Francisco, CA: McGraw-Hill.

Fowler, Mary. 1999. *Maybe You Know My Kid: A Parent's Guide to Helping Your Child with Attention-Deficit Hyperactivity Disorder*. Secaucus, NJ: Carol Publishing Group.

Glang, Ann; George Singer; and Bonnie Todis. 1997. *Students with Acquired Brain Injury: The School's Response*. Baltimore, Maryland: Paul H. Brookes Publishing Company.

Gronwall, Dorothy; Philip Wrightson; & Peter Waddell. 1997. *Head Injury: The Facts*. New York, NY: Oxford University Press.

Harnad, Stevan (Ed.). 1998. *Behavioral and Brain Sciences: An International Journal of Current Research and Theory with Open Peer Commentary*. Dec.; Volume 21 (6). Port Chester, NY: Cambridge University Press.

Hurford, Daphne. 1998. *To Read or Not to Read*. New York, NY: Scribner.

Karr-Morse, Robin & Meredith Wiley. 1997. *Ghosts from the Nursery: Tracing the Roots of Violence*. New York, NY: Atlantic Monthly Press.

Kellerman, Jonathan. 1999. *Savage Spawn: Reflections on Violent Children*. New York, NY: The Ballantine Publishing Group.

Llinas, Rodolfo. 1990. *The Workings of the Brain: Development, Memory, and Perception*. New York, NY: W. H. Freeman & Company.

Lyon, G. Reid & Judith Rumsey. 1996. *Neuroimaging: A Window to the Neurological Foundations of Learning and Behavior in Children*. Baltimore, Maryland: Paul H. Brookes Publishing Company.

Maria, Bernard. 1999. *Current Management in Child Neurology*. Hamilton, London: B. C. Decker, Inc.

Mazziotta, John; Arthur Toga; & Richard Frackowiak. 2000. *Brain Mapping the Disorders*. San Diego, CA: Academic Press.

McEwen, Bruce & Harold Schmeck, Jr. 1994. *The Hostage Brain*. New York, NY: The Rockefeller University Press.

Morrison, James. 1995. *DSM-IV Made Easy: The Clinician's Guide to Diagnosis*. New York, NY: The Guilford Press.

Niehoff, Debra. 1999. *The Biology of Violence: How Understanding the Brain, Behavior, and Environment Can Break the Victims Circle of Aggression*. New York, NY: Simon & Schuster.

Olivier, Carolyn & Rosemary F. Bowler. 1996. *Learning to Learn*. New York, NY: Simon & Schuster.

Perry, Susanna. 1999. *Abnormal Psychology*. Chicago, Illinois: NTC/Contemporary Publishing Group.

Peterson, Christopher; Steven Maier; and Martin Seligman. 1993. *Learned Helplessness: A Theory for the Age of Personal Control*. New York, NY: Oxford University Press.

Posner, Michael & Marcus Raichle. 1994. *Images of Mind*. New York, NY: Scientific American Library.

Radetsky, Peter. 1997. *Allergic to the Twentieth Century*. New York, NY: Little Brown & Company.

Reichenberg-Ullman, Judyth & Robert Ullman. 1996. *Ritalin-Free Kids: Safe and Effective Homeopathic Medicine for ADD and Other Behavioral and Learning Problems*. Rocklin, CA: Prima Publishing.

Ruden, Ronald & Marcia Byalick. 1997. *The Craving Brain: The Biobalance Approach to Controlling Addictions*. New York, NY: HarperCollins.

Sapolksy, Robert. 1998. *Why Zebras Don't Get Ulcers: An Updated Guide to Stress, Stress-Related Diseases, and Coping*. New York, NY: W. H. Freeman & Company.

Schwartz, Jeffrey. 1997. *Brain Lock*. New York, NY: HarperCollins Publishers.

Silver, Daniel & Michael Rosenbluth. 1992. *Handbook of Borderline Disorders*. Madison, CT: International Universities Press, Inc.

Snyder, Solomon. 1996. *Drugs and the Brain*. New York, NY: Scientific American Library.

Turkington, Carol. 1996. *The Brain Encyclopedia*. New York, NY: Facts On File, Inc.

Valenstein, Elliot. 1998. *Blaming the Brain: The Truth About Drugs and Mental Health*. New York, NY: The Free Press/Simon & Schuster.

Reader Resources

Books on Learning, Teaching, and the Brain

The Brain Store features countless books, posters, CDs, and brain-related products. This innovative education resource company is all about the science of learning. You'll find resources for:

- **Teaching and Training**
- **Enrichment**
- **Staff Development**
- **Music and Dance**
- **Organizational Change**
- **Early Childhood**

To view all of our products, log on at: **www.thebrainstore.com**, or call (800) 325-4769 or (858) 546-7555 for a FREE color resource catalog.

Monthly Newsletter: The LearningBrain

Stay up to date with the newest and most relevant information on learning topics like environments, nutrition, arts, memory, school policy, mind-body, skill transfer, and fragile brains. Save hundreds of hours in research time and expense. Gain twenty-first century teaching and training strategies. To get a free sample issue, log on at: **www.learningbrain.com** or call (800) 325-4769 or (858) 546-7555.

Conference: The Learning Brain Expo

A world-class gathering featuring more than fifty renowned speakers on the brain and learning. Session topics include music, movement, early childhood, emotions, memory, the fragile brain, and brain imaging. Get dozens of practical ideas and network with like-minded professionals. Held twice annually, you can attend this enriching event in either California or Texas. For more information, log on at: **www.brainexpo.com**, or call (800) 325-4769 or (858) 546-7555.

Free Samples

Go to **www.thebrainstore.com** to get free tips, tools, and strategies. You'll also find selected products at 40 percent savings. In addition, many books offer you a sneak online preview of the table of contents and sample pages so you'll know before you order if it's for you. At The Brain Store, online shopping is safe, quick, and easy!

About the Author

Eric Jensen, M.A. is a visionary educator who is committed to making a positive, significant, and lasting difference in the way we learn. He's a member of the prestigious Society for Neuroscience and New York Academy of Sciences. A former middle-school teacher and college instructor, Jensen is the author of more than a dozen books on learning and teaching. He co-founded the world's first experimental brain-compatible academic enrichment program in 1982 that now has more than 30,000 graduates. Currently, he's a staff developer and consultant living in San Diego, California.

Other Books by Eric Jensen

Super Teaching, Student Success Secrets, The Learning Brain, Brain-Based Learning, Trainer's Bonanza, Teaching with the Brain in Mind, Joyful Fluency (with Lynn Dhority), *The Great Memory Book* (with Karen Markowitz), *Learning with the Body in Mind*, and *Different Brains, Different Learners*. Available through The Brain Store. Log on at: **www.thebrainstore.com**, or call (800) 325-4769 or (858) 546-7555.

Trainings Facilitated by Eric Jensen

"How the Brain Learns" is a 6-day workshop for teachers, trainers, and other change agents with a focus on the brain, how we learn, and how to boost achievement.
"The Fragile Brain" is 3-day program for teachers, special educators, counselors, and other change agents with a focus on what can go wrong with the learner's brain and how to treat it.
For registration information, dates, and costs call (888) 638-7246 or fax (858) 642-0404.

Author Contact

Fax (858) 642-0404 or e-mail at eric@jlcbrain.com

Index

MANY PEOPLE THINK TROLLS ARE LIKE GNOMES: TINY CHUBBY people wearing red pointed caps. Others think trolls are little plastic toys with pink or orange hair. Norwegian trolls, which are the first trolls, aren't like that at all. They're giants. They can be so big that their heads loom above the tallest treetops. In fact, they are so big that they have to live inside mountains or under really tall bridges.

Trolls are ugly to look at. Their eyes can be the size of potlids, and their noses as long as rake handles. Not only that, trolls love to eat children or little animals. Fortunately, the brain inside that huge head is tiny. Even a little goat can figure out how to outsmart a troll.

The Three Billy Goats Gruff

ONCE UPON A TIME, a long long time ago, way up in the mountains of Norway, there lived three goats and the names of all three were The Billy Goats Gruff. Now these goats needed to go up into the mountains in the summertime because that's where the grass was greenest. But in order to get there they had to cross an enormous bridge, and underneath that bridge lived a huge hideous troll. His eyes were as big as pewter plates and his nose as long as a poker. But there was no way around it. Across the bridge they had to go.

The first one to cross the bridge was the teeniest tiniest of the three billy goats. When he walked across the bridge it made a little sound like this:

Tripp, trapp

Tripp, trapp

"WHO'S THAT STEPPING ON MY BRIDGE?" roared the troll.

"Oh, it's only me. I'm the teeniest, tiniest of the Three Billy Goats Gruff and I'm on my way up into the mountains to get fat," whispered the little goat in his little goat voice.

"WELL, I'M COMING TO GOBBLE YOU UP NOW," roared the troll.

"Oh, please don't eat me up. If you wait a little longer my brother will come and he is much bigger and fatter than I am."

"OH, ALL RIGHT THEN," huffed the troll. And the little goat ran away as fast as he could.

The next one to cross the bridge was the second of the three billy goats, and when he walked across the bridge it made a sound like this:

TRIPP, TRAPP

TRIPP, TRAPP

"WHO'S THAT STEPPING ACROSS MY BRIDGE?" shouted the troll.

"It's mmm . . . me, the sss . . . second of the Three BBBB . . . Billy Goats GG . . . Gruff and I'm on mmm . . . my way to the mountains to get fat," stammered the goat in a shaking voice.

"WELL, I'M COMING TO GOBBLE YOU UP NOW," bellowed the troll.

"Oh, ppp . . . please don't eat me up. Why don't you wait a little while till my bbb . . . brother comes. He's much bigger and fatter . . . and tastier too."

"ALL RIGHT THEN," roared the troll and the little goat ran across the bridge as fast as his little legs would go.

Now the next one to walk across the bridge was the biggest of the three billy goats. His fur was shimmering and shining and on his head were two gigantic horns. He was so heavy that when he walked across the bridge it sounded like thunder:

TRIPP, TRAPP

TRIPP, TRAPP

"WHO'S THAT STEPPING ON MY BRIDGE?" roared the troll, for now he was really hungry.

"It's **ME**. I'm the biggest of The Three Billy Goats Gruff and I'm on my way up into the mountains to get fat," boomed the goat in his deep voice.

"WELL I'M COMING TO GOBBLE YOU UP NOW."

"Why don't you come along," the goat taunted.

"I've got two spears,

With those I'll poke out your eyeballs at your ears.

I've got hooves as strong as stones,

With those I'll break your body and your bones."

And he went at the troll and broke every bone in his body and poked his eyes out and sent him way down into the river. Then he went with his brothers up into the mountains, where they ate and got so big and so fat, that if the fat hasn't fallen off them yet, why, they're still there.

Snipp, snapp, snute (snip, snup, snoo-TA)

Her er eventyret ute! (haer aer ayvan-TEER-a ooTA)

Snip, snap, snout,
This tale's told out!

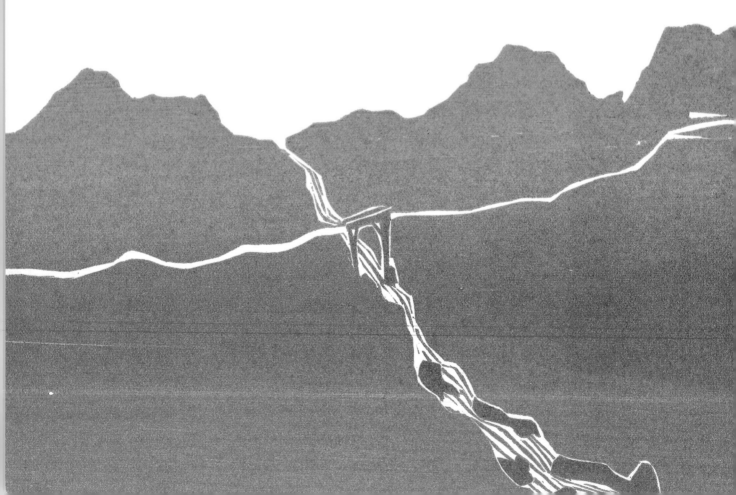

This story is from Asbjørnsen and Moe, "De Tre Bukkene Bruse Som gikk til Seters For å Gjøre seg Fete." This is the best known Norwegian folktale. In fact, I believe that in the 1950s it was voted the most popular story among American children. Frequently, when speaking with adults about trolls, they say, "Well I know they live under bridges." My version is substantially like the Norwegian version. There is not much one can do to improve a story as good as this one. It is the first story I told in English.

ALL TROLLS ARE UGLY, BUT THE UGLIEST OF ALL ARE THE TROLLS with three, six, or nine heads. They get terrible headaches, probably from the different heads arguing with each other, and the only thing that can soothe them is being gently rubbed by the hands of a princess. That's why trolls often steal princesses and keep them captive inside their mountain homes. To figure out how to get rescued from a troll, you have to know their greatest weakness. Trolls, you see, think they are very smart, and they love to brag about how clever they are. The prince and princess in this story know that if they can make the trolls boast, they may give away important clues. They also know that if the sun shines directly on a troll, he will burst and turn to stone.

The Boy Who Became a Lion, a Falcon, and an Ant

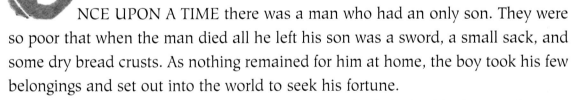

ONCE UPON A TIME there was a man who had an only son. They were so poor that when the man died all he left his son was a sword, a small sack, and some dry bread crusts. As nothing remained for him at home, the boy took his few belongings and set out into the world to seek his fortune.

His way lay across a mountain, and when he had climbed high enough to get a view of his surroundings, he spotted a lion, a falcon, and an ant quarreling over a dead horse. The boy was frightened at the sight of the lion and wanted to hide. The lion saw him, however, and called for him to come and settle their quarrel. The boy went over and took a good look. Then he pulled out his sword and divided the horse as best he could.

To the lion he gave the large joints, saying, "The lion should have the most, for he is the biggest and strongest." Then he gave the liver and the tasty tidbits to the falcon. "The falcon should have the tastiest bits, for he is such a dainty eater." Last he gave the head to the ant, "For he likes creeping in nooks and crannies," he said.

The three animals were so pleased with the clever way the boy had divided the

horse that they wanted to reward him. But the boy just smiled. "If I have helped you, that is reward enough for me."

Still the animals insisted. "If there is nothing else you want, perhaps you would like three wishes?" the lion finally said. The boy liked that idea, but he could not think of what to wish for.

"Would you like to be able to turn into a lion?" asked the lion.

"And a falcon?" said the falcon.

"And an ant?" added the ant.

The boy thought this might be useful so he made the wishes.

Immediately, he threw away his sword and sack and turned himself into a falcon. He bristled his new wings, tested them on the wind a few times, and took off. He flew over mountains and valleys and forests. As he flew over a large lake his wings became so sore he could hardly fly on. At last he spotted a huge rocky crag in the lake and landed there. It was an odd-looking rock, jagged and rough and with a large outcropping on one side. Being curious, he changed himself into an ant and spent some time exploring it.

After he had rested he became a falcon again and flew all the way to the king's farm. There he landed on a branch outside the princess's window. When she saw the bird she thought it so beautiful that she wanted to keep it. She coaxed it to her and as soon as the bird was in her room, she slammed the window shut, and locked it in a cage.

But the boy was not worried. When night came, he just turned himself into an ant and crawled out of the cage. Then he became a boy again and went and sat down by the sleeping princess. She awoke and screamed with fright, but the boy calmed her.

"Why do you scream so? I'm not going to hurt you."

"I thought you were the troll I have been promised to."

"How in the world did you get promised to a troll?" asked the boy.

"Two other trolls have already stolen my sisters," said the princess, "and now a horrible monster with nine heads wants me for his bride or he will destroy my father's kingdom. Every Thursday the troll sends his messenger, a dragon with nine heads. My father has managed to hold him off by feeding him pigs, one for each head. Now there are almost no pigs left in the entire kingdom and I am scared to walk outside."

When the boy heard this he was determined to battle the dragon.

The very next morning he went to the king and told him. The king was well pleased, and as it happened to be Thursday the boy immediately set out for the field where the dragon came to receive his pigs.

Soon enough, a huge serpentine shape with enormous webbed wings lashed the air. Its nine heads spouted fiery flames as it swooped down. When there was no sight of its meal it roared and spat, then lifted its enormous body and charged at the boy as if it was going to swallow him alive. In a twinkling the boy became a lion, reared up on his hind legs, and leaped at the dragon, sinking his teeth deep into the scaly body.

The lion tore off one head after another till at last only the ninth head was left. But that was the strongest head. In its mouth were nine forked tongues, and it spouted blazing venom as it lashed its mighty tail and attacked. But the lion was

SMALL BUSHES AND TREES OFTEN GROW ON TOP OF TROLLS' HEADS. As the trolls get older more shrubs and bushes grow until the trolls themselves begin to look like old trees. The trolls shrink, too, and sometimes become tiny. Some of the meanness goes out of them with age, but they can still be awfully tricky.

Next time you're out for a walk in the woods, look for dead trees, especially overturned tree roots. They might well be trolls that died of old age instead of bursting and becoming stone. Study them carefully and you might spot eye sockets, arms, and a nose (it'll be long). They might look a little like the trolls in this story.

The Handshake

THERE WAS ONCE a man named Haakon (HO-kun) who lost his horse in the mountains. He searched in every crack and crevice, but could not find it. All of a sudden a fog rolled in. It was so thick that Haakon couldn't even see his hand in front of his face. For hours he wandered in the fog until finally he found himself in a pasture.

"I thought there was nothing but rocks and boggy hollows up here," Haakon muttered to himself. Nevertheless, in front of him lay a lush green pasture and at the far end of it, he saw a farm with many buildings. Outside stood an old fellow chopping wood, so Haakon went over to him and asked if he had seen his horse.

"You must ask my father," said the man. "He's sitting by the hearth."

Haakon went inside and there he saw an even older and smaller person cooking bacon over the fire. His whole body was trembling and shaking, and he looked like an old, dry spruce tree all covered with lichen and moss. Again Haakon asked if this fellow had seen the horse, but he replied, "You must ask my father. He's inside the horn you see hanging there on the wall."

Surprised, Haakon looked over at the wall, and there hung a mighty big horn, and inside the horn sat a man who was so old that he could neither see nor walk.

THE NEXT STORY IS ONE OF MY FAVORITES BECAUSE IT HAS A female troll, called a troll hag, and she doesn't carry her head on top of her shoulders. Instead she carries it underneath her arm. Imagine how scary it would be to hear her deep rumbling voice coming from her armpit! Troll hags are a little different from trolls. They're usually smaller, they can be out in the sun without bursting, and they're quite a bit smarter than the trolls. You have to really use your brain to outwit a troll hag, as this story shows you.

Butterball

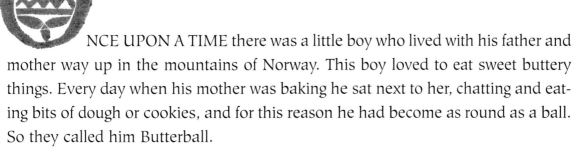

NCE UPON A TIME there was a little boy who lived with his father and mother way up in the mountains of Norway. This boy loved to eat sweet buttery things. Every day when his mother was baking he sat next to her, chatting and eating bits of dough or cookies, and for this reason he had become as round as a ball. So they called him Butterball.

One day the mother was baking and Butterball was eating just as usual, when suddenly their dog, Goldtooth, barked loudly. "Butterball, go out and see why Goldtooth is barking so," said the mother. Butterball ran outside. A hideous sight met his eyes. Down from the mountain strode a large troll hag. She carried her head under her left arm, and sticks and root tips protruded from her neck where her head should have been! In her right hand she clutched a large burlap sack.

"Mom, Mom," Butterball wailed. "There's a troll hag coming down the mountain. What shall we do?"

"Quick! Go and hide underneath my baking table. Stay quiet and let me handle everything," said Butterball's mother calmly. "OK," said Butterball and crept underneath the table.

Soon the door shook from loud knocks. "Come in," called Butterball's mother sweetly. The troll hag stooped and squeezed through the doorway.

"Good day. Is Butterball at home today?" rumbled the troll hag from beneath her armpit.

"Oh, I'm so sorry!" said Butterball's mother. "He's out hunting grouse with his father today. It's too bad you missed him."

"Yes, that's too bad," agreed the troll hag, her wicked little eyes darting around the room, "because I have this beautiful little silver knife that I so wanted to give him."

"**Pip, pip!** Here I am," said Butterball and shot out from beneath the table.

"Oh, Butterball, there you are! My back is so sore. Why don't you crawl into the sack and collect the knife yourself?"

Butterball didn't need to be asked twice. He dove into the sack, but no sooner was he inside than the troll hag grabbed the sack, flung it over her shoulder, and rushed out the door.

She had walked for a long time when she finally grew tired and dropped the sack on the road.

"I'm going to take a little nap. Why don't you take one too, and then we'll be on our way," said the troll hag. Soon Butterball heard hacking noises in the forest. The ground shook from the troll hag's snores. Quickly he found the silver knife, sliced a hole in the sack, and escaped. In the forest he found a root about the same size that he was, which he rolled into the sack so it looked as though he was still there. Then he ran home as fast as he could.

The troll hag was fuming with anger when she came home, opened her sack, and discovered the root, so the next day exactly the same thing happened. Butterball and his mother were baking when Goldtooth started barking. Again Butterball ran outside, and again he came right in. "Oh, Mom, that hag is coming back and she's uglier than ever. What shall we do?"

"You know perfectly well what we are going to do. Get under the table, stay still, and don't make a peep, and everything will be all right," replied his mother. Butterball did as his mother told him, and soon there was a loud knock on the door.

"Good day. Is Butterball at home today?" rasped the troll hag's voice from beneath her armpit.

"I'm sorry, but Butterball is out hunting grouse with his father today," said the mother.

"That's too bad," said the hag in her husky voice. "I have this beautiful little silver fork that I so wanted to give to him."

"**Pip, pip!** Here I am," said Butterball, and again he came scooting out from under the table.

"Butterball, my back is still bad. Why don't you crawl into the sack yourself."

He did, and as soon as he was inside, the troll hag grabbed the sack, flung it over her shoulder, and rushed off. Once again the troll hag grew tired and stopped for a nap. As soon as Butterball heard the snores he grabbed the fork and began to

make a hole. It was a little more difficult, but he finally made a small hole. He tore a bigger opening with his fingers and crawled out. This time he found a big round rock to put in the sack in place of himself.

When the troll hag came home she broke her best pot when she dropped the rock into it. Now she was almost trembling with anger.

The third day was just like the others. Goldtooth started to bark and Butterball ran out to see who it was. He came back as fast as his little legs would carry him.

"Mom, oh, mercy me! It's the hag again. What are we to do?"

"Butterball!" said his mother in a stern voice. "You know perfectly well what to do. Crawl under my baking table and stay there. Whatever happens, don't come out and don't make a peep. Now will you promise to listen to me?"

"All right, I'll do just as you say," said Butterball and crawled under the table.

"Good day," said the troll hag's head from beneath the armpit as she squeezed through the door. "Is Butterball at home today?"

"Indeed he is not," said the mother. "He is out in the woods hunting grouse with his father."

"That's too bad," said the hag, "for I have such a pretty little silver spoon to give him."

"**Pip, pip!** Here I am!" said Butterball and again he jumped out from underneath the table.

"My back is still so stiff, Butterball. You'll have to fetch the spoon for yourself."

Butterball squatted and crept into the sack. No sooner was he inside than the troll hag grabbed the sack, flung it over her shoulders, and strode off. This time she didn't stop until she reached her house. There she called her daughter.

"Now daughter," drooled the troll hag, "you must cook stew out of this juicy Butterball while I'm away fetching your father. When we get back we shall have a feast."

After the troll hag left, the troll daughter wanted to cook Butterball, but she wasn't quite sure how to go about doing it, being neither very clever nor used to cooking. Butterball saw her confusion and said, "I can help you. I know how to cook. I cook with my mom every day."

"Oh, good," said the troll daughter, her mouth already watering at the thought of stew. Butterball explained about pots and pans, fire and water, and finally, the pot and the water were ready.

"Now you have to test the water to see if it is warm enough," said Butterball.

"Huh? How do I do that?" The troll daughter was now so hungry for Butterball stew that slobber ran down her chin.

"Lift the pot lid and plunge your hand into the water."

"How do I know if it is hot?" whined the troll daughter.

"If it burns a little, it's ready," said Butterball.

"Oh, I knew that!" said the troll daughter.

She leaned over the pot and was just about to stick her hand into the water when Butterball bent his head down as if he were a billy goat, took a running start, and butted the troll daughter's behind so hard that into the pot she tipped!

Then he slammed on the lid and ran out of the house and into the forest, where he found the root and the rock and dragged them onto the ledge above the door. He scrambled up after them and waited quietly. In the distance he heard trees being knocked over and rocks being crushed. Soon both the troll and the hag stood in the doorway, their giant noses sniffing the air excitedly.

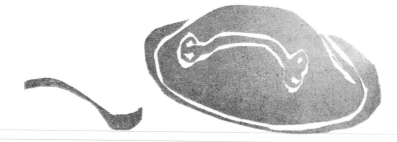

"You're looking for your horse I reckon," squeaked the ancient man. "We had to shut it in the stable for it got into our field. It has suffered no harm. But where are you from?"

"I'm from Seljord," said Haakon.

At that the old man brightened and asked excitedly, "Are folks in Seljord as strong now as they were in the old days? Give me your hand to shake so I can see if you have proper marrow in your fingers."

Haakon reached out to shake the wizened old hand, when the man by the hearth tugged at his sleeve.

"If you want your hand back in one piece, you'd better give him this iron bar instead," he whispered.

"Ha!" shouted the ancient one and squeezed the iron bar so hard that water oozed from it. "There's nothing but sheep's milk in the fingers of folks from Seljord nowadays. It was different in the old days. Haven't you heard of me? I'm called Skaane and I helped St. Olav build the church in Seljord."

"But it's been several hundred years now since St. Olav built that church," said Haakon. "And if you helped him, why are you living in this lonely place?"

"When the big bell came to the church I had to move out here. I couldn't stand the sound. I was strong, but St. Olav was stronger than me."

When Haakon was leaving, the old men handed over his horse. Haakon could scarcely recognize it, so fat and sleek had it become. "I told you it had suffered no harm," creaked the ancient one. In return for the good treatment Haakon had to promise not to look behind him, but hurry back the same way he had come.

"Good-bye then," said the old man.

"Good-bye yourself," said Haakon and seated himself on the horse. But riding across the pasture he could not resist one last look at the farm. He turned around after all, and the farm was gone! Where the pasture and the farm buildings had stood was the big mountain. It was as black and gray as it had always been, and now Haakon knew that it was trolls he had visited.

Snipp, snapp, snute
Her er eventyret ute!

Snip, snap, snout,
This tale's told out!

This story is based on a tale from Folktales of Norway, *edited by Reidar Christiansen, translated by Pat Shaw Iversen, University of Chicago Press, 1964. It is titled "The Old Troll and the Handshake." The story is a wonderful example of how trolls supposedly helped build a number of churches until St. Olav, the patron saint of Norway, drove them into hiding. There are many local legends on this theme, but this is by far the most interesting one to people outside of Norway. Usually the stories involve trolls turning into stone after their work is done, explaining some local, odd rock formations. In this story, the trolls have withdrawn into an elusive world, parallel to, but not easily accessible from ours. Thus we learn that trolls are still among us, but not encountered as readily as in the old days.*

Trolls are not only bullies, but thieves too. Besides trying to eat children and goats, they love to steal gold and silver, or better yet, things that are magical. The troll hag in this story is very greedy and sneaky, so it takes the boy some time before he figures out how to use the gifts from the North Wind properly.

The Boy and the North Wind

Once upon a time there was a boy named Per who lived with his mother way up in the mountains of Norway. One day Per's mother asked him to fetch flour for bread and cookies. Happily, Per grabbed the biggest bowl he could find and went to the barn. He filled the bowl all the way to the brim and ran back across the yard when suddenly — *whoosh* — the North Wind gusted around the corner and blew all the flour away.

Per returned to the barn, filled the bowl, and hurried back across the yard when — *whoosh* — again the North Wind came and blew the flour away. Once more Per went to the barn. He took all the flour that was left, which wasn't even enough to fill the bowl. He cradled it carefully and hurried across the yard. But — *whoosh* — came the North Wind around the corner and blew all the flour away.

"That means gruel the rest of the winter," scolded Per's mother. "No bread and certainly no cookies until next year."

"What! No bread or cookies? I'm getting the flour back," Per declared and, before his mother could stop him, out the door he went.

All day he trudged through the snow until finally he came to the place where the North Wind lived. "North Wind! You better come out here. I've got to talk to you," Per called, knocking on the door as loudly as he could.

After several minutes the North Wind opened the door. He rubbed his eyes and yawned, "What's all this knocking and hollering about? I can't nap with all this noise around."

"You stole our flour!" Per burst out. "You came to our house three times today

and blew all our flour away, and because of you we won't have any bread all winter. We'll probably starve and it'll be your fault."

The North Wind's face wrinkled up. "Oh, I'm really sorry," he said in his deep booming voice. "Sometimes I get carried away with all my blowing. I don't mean any harm, but there is no way now that I can get the flour back for you." He looked at the boy for a minute. Then he added, "I can't get the flour back, but I can get something else."

He went inside and came back with a cloth. "This cloth is magic. All you have to do is say: 'Cloth, cloth, spread yourself and bring forth wonderful food,' and you will have all the food and drink you'll ever need."

Per thanked the North Wind, took the cloth, and set off. It was almost nighttime. Along the road was an inn where Per decided to spend the night. He knocked at the door and immediately it swung open. Out stepped a troll hag with a nose so long she had tucked it into her belt to keep from tripping.

"Good evening," said the hag in a hoarse voice.

"Good evening," stammered Per. "I was wondering if I could have a bed for tonight?"

"How are you going to pay for it?" rumbled the troll hag.

"I haven't any money, but I could feed you and your guests."

"How?" demanded the troll hag.

Per grabbed each end of the cloth, shook it and said, "Cloth, cloth, spread yourself and bring forth wonderful food."

Instantly the cloth was filled: roasts and chops, meatballs and sausages, vegetables and fruits, pies and puddings, and glorious things to drink.

When all the guests at the inn had their fill, Per rolled up his cloth and went to bed. In the middle of the night, when everyone was sleeping, that troll hag came sneaking up the stairs with a cloth that looked exactly like Per's. She tiptoed into his room and exchanged her cloth for his.

In the morning when Per woke up he grabbed the cloth and ran home. "Mom, Mom, look what the North Wind gave me," he shouted excitedly. Quickly he said the magic words and shook out the cloth. Nothing happened! Again and again he tried, holding the cloth upside down or in different ways, but nothing worked.

"The North Wind has tricked me," Per muttered angrily and stomped off to the North Wind's house before his mom could stop him.

"North Wind! You'd better come out here. I've got to talk to you," Per hollered at the door. After a bit the North Wind came out, rubbing his eyes sleepily.

"You again?" he yawned. "Why are you back so soon?"

"You know why I'm back," Per shouted, almost in tears. "That cloth you gave me, it's no good. It only worked once, and what use is that?"

"Only once? Something is wrong," said the North Wind. "But let's not argue. I'll give you something else." Soon he returned with a ram.

"This is a magic ram. All you have to do is say, 'Ram, ram make money,' and it will make all the money you need."

"Will it work more than once?" Per asked suspiciously.

"Forever," promised the North Wind.

Per took the goat and set off. But it was getting late so he decided to go back to the inn. As soon as he knocked, the troll hag flung open the door. This time soup was dripping from her enormous nose for she'd been using it to stir her pot.

"Good evening. I was wondering if I could have a bed for the night," asked Per.

"How are you going to pay?" growled the hag.

Per turned to the ram and said, "Ram, ram, make money." Instantly, out of its mouth dropped a heap of gold coins. Per paid the hag, spent another coin on food, and then went to bed. In the middle of the night, again the troll hag tiptoed up the stairs, this time with her own ram, which she exchanged for his.

When Per returned home he tried to show his mother what the ram could make. But this ram, if it made anything at all, it surely wasn't money!

Per stormed back to the North Wind, even angrier than before. The North Wind just scratched his big frosty head, shook it, and said, "Something has gone wrong. I'll get one last thing for you, but you'd better use it wisely." He went inside and returned with a stick. "This stick is also magic. All you have to do is say, 'Stick, stick, lay on,' and it will beat anyone you want. When you want it to stop, just say, 'Stick, stick, stop beating,' and it will come right back to you."

Per thanked the North Wind and again he went back to the inn.

"Good day," greeted the troll hag.

"Could I have a bed for the night?"

"How do you plan to pay for it?" grunted the troll hag, eyeing the stick. Per fished some leftover coins from his pocket, and this time he went straight to bed.

In the middle of the night, again the hag came sneaking up the stairs. She was sure the stick had some kind of magic. Slowly she tiptoed into the room. Just as

she was about to exchange her stick for his, Per jumped up and yelled, "Stick, stick, lay on."

The stick flew from the pillow and started to beat that troll hag so thoroughly that she hopped from one foot to the other, over chairs and under tables, yowling and yelling, until finally she screamed, "Make it stop, make it stop!"

"Not until you give me back my cloth and my ram," shouted Per.

"I will, I will," screamed the troll hag.

"Stick, stick, stop beating," commanded Per and immediately the stick flew back into his hand. But he kept it safely in his hand as he marched behind the troll hag to fetch his cloth and his ram.

The next day Per returned home with his treasures, and with them he and his mother had all the food and money and protection they needed to the end of their days.

Snipp, snapp, snute
Her er eventyret ute!

Snip, snap, snout,
This tale's told out!

From Asbjørnsen and Moe, "Gutten Som Gikk til Norden-vinden og Krevde Igjen Melet." The version I tell is inspired by my father's vigorous retelling. It has some differences from the original, most notably in the description of the troll hag. In the Norwegian she is not actually a troll hag, but an old crone. My father made her into a troll hag, and I, inspired by a wonderful drawing the Norwegian illustrator Theodore Kittelsen did of a troll hag in the late 1800s, added the enormously long nose with stew dripping from it.

TROLLS LOVE TO EAT, BUT THEY ARE USUALLY TOO LAZY TO COOK A good meal for themselves. During the holiday season, with lots of good food around, they sometimes travel in packs to scare people into giving them food. Then you really get to see what terrible manners trolls have, especially the troll children. They love to fight over the food and they don't even know how to use a knife and a fork! When I had bad manners, my mother called me *"en trollunge,"* a troll child, to remind me that human nature and manners are far different from the trolls'.

The White Cat in the Dovre Mountain

ONCE UPON A TIME there was a man who caught a big white bear, which he wanted to take as a gift to the king. He happened to cross the Dovre Mountains on Christmas Eve, and there he found a cottage where he asked for shelter for himself and the white bear.

"Heavens no!" exclaimed the farmer, who was named Halvor. "We can't put you up. We can't even stay here ourselves tonight."

"How so?" asked the man with the white bear.

"Every Christmas Eve such a pack of trolls descends on us that we dare not stay. They eat all our food and sleep in our beds and won't leave until every cupboard has been emptied."

"Is that all?" said the man. "I still think you can put me up. My bear can sleep under the stove there and a closet will do for me."

"Suit yourself," said Halvor, "but we're leaving."

Halvor, his wife, and all their children left, and the man and his white bear made themselves comfortable. The house was snug and warm, the tables laden with all the good foods necessary for a feast: sausages and meatballs, fish and chicken, porridge and pie. The man sampled a little of everything, and then he and the white bear settled down for the night.

All at once the air filled with a dreadful stomping, snorting, and screaming as

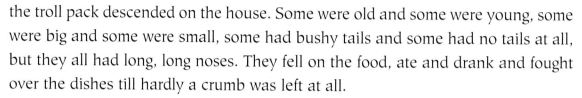

the troll pack descended on the house. Some were old and some were young, some were big and some were small, some had bushy tails and some had no tails at all, but they all had long, long noses. They fell on the food, ate and drank and fought over the dishes till hardly a crumb was left at all.

The man was awake inside the broom closet and watched everything through a crack in the door. He saw two little trolls fighting over a fat sausage.

"It's mine. I saw it first," screamed one little troll and whapped at the other with his tail.

"No it isn't! I grabbed it before you. It's mine, mine, MINE!" hollered the other little troll even louder and kicked the first troll as hard as he could.

Screaming and tearing at each other, both little trolls pulled at the sausage when, suddenly, it slipped out of their hands and rolled onto the floor, right to the stove where the white bear was sleeping. The man watched as both trolls dropped down and started to search under the tables.

YOU HAVE ALREADY LEARNED SOME GOOD WAYS TO TRICK TROLLS, such as making them brag and give away their secrets. The main thing is to stay calm, be brave, and use your head. Trolls are awfully slow thinkers. If you keep remembering how much smarter humans are than trolls, you should be able to outwit even the largest trolls just as the Ashlad does in this story.

The Eating Competition

NCE UPON A TIME there was a farmer who had three sons. On their farm was a large forest where the farmer often went to cut wood. With the wood he built many wonderful things and provided well for his family.

One day the farmer hurt his back. For weeks he stayed in bed, and after some time the family ran out of money. The farmer tried to get his sons to help, but they were lazy and wouldn't turn their hands to do a thing.

"Oh, Pa," they complained. "You'll be up and about soon. What do you need our help for? We don't like the woods. There are trolls there."

"Trolls," scoffed the farmer. "I knew what to do with them even when I was a little lad. Here you are, nearly grown and still afraid."

The father kept pleading with his sons, and after some time, he finally got them around to his way of thinking. Per, the oldest, was the first one to go. He was a big burly fellow and swaggered off into the woods.

After a bit he came to a spot where some tall, shaggy spruce grew so he rolled up his sleeves, grabbed his ax, and got ready to cut. No sooner had he struck the first blow than out of the forest charged a huge, monstrous troll.

His eyes blazed as he roared, "If you're cutting down my wood I'll kill you and eat you!"

Per got so scared, he just flung his ax aside and took to his heels. When he came home he was panting and sobbing. "You don't know how lucky you are that I am still alive. I met this horrible troll out in the woods and he wanted to kill me and eat me," he wailed.

"What!" exclaimed his father. "You ran away from a troll! Don't you know those creatures are stupid? When I was your age I dealt with trolls all the time. But you, you're behaving like a chicken!"

The next day the second son, Paul, set out, and he fared no better than Per. As soon as he struck the first blow the troll burst out of the forest.

"If you're cutting down my trees, I'll kill you and eat you!" Paul took one look at the troll, tossed his ax aside, and fled as fast as he could. When he got home he was completely out of breath and sobbing like a baby.

"Oh, you don't know how lucky you are that I'm still alive. There was a huge troll out there ready to kill me and eat me."

"Bah," snorted the father. "I can't believe you're scared of a troll. When I was your age, I battled trolls all the time. But you, you're nothing but a chicken."

On the third day the youngest was to set out. He was nicknamed the Ashlad because he spent so much time poking around in the fireplace. When the brothers saw him get ready they burst out laughing.

"What? You go out into the woods? You've hardly been beyond the front door and now you think you're ready to take on a troll?" But the Ashlad paid them no heed. Instead he went to his mother and asked for some provisions. There wasn't much food left, but she gave him a bag of homemade cheese. This he put in a knapsack, picked up his ax, and strode off.

After a bit he, too, came to the place where the large spruce grew and got ready to cut. No sooner had he struck the first blow when out of the woods the troll came screaming and roaring, "If you're cutting down my wood, I'm going to kill you and eat you."

But this boy, he wasn't slow! Quickly he ran to his knapsack, pulled out a large lump of cheese, and squeezed it in his hands until the water squirted. "If you don't watch out," he shouted, "I'm going to squeeze you the way I'm squeezing the water out of this white rock in my hand."

When the troll saw that he got frightened, "Nay, my dear fellow, spare me! I had no idea you were so strong. I'll help you chop," he whimpered.

Well, on that condition the Ashlad agreed to spare him, and the troll was so clever at woodcutting that in a short time they had felled many cords of wood. Evening was drawing near when they finished. All at once the troll looked hungrily at the boy. "How about if you come to my place to have a bite to eat? My place is closer than yours."

The Ashlad said yes and off they went. When they arrived at the mountain where the troll lived, the troll said, "I'll make up the fire. Why don't you get water from the well so we can make porridge?" The boy agreed, but when he went to fetch the water buckets he found they were of solid iron and so huge and heavy that he couldn't so much as budge them. "It's not worth collecting water from these tiny thimbles you have here. I'm going to fetch the entire well, I am!" the Ashlad shouted to the troll.

"Nay, nay, my dear fellow," hollered the troll in dismay. "I can't lose my well. Let's switch tasks. You make the fire and I'll go after the water."

That's what they did, and the troll cooked up a huge pot of porridge. When they were ready to eat, the Ashlad noticed the troll eyeing him hungrily. With a flash in his eyes he suddenly suggested, "If it's all the same to you, let's have an eating competition."

SOME TROLLS DON'T CARRY THEIR HEARTS IN THEIR BODIES, BUT keep them carefully hidden. To defeat such a troll, you need all the help you can get, for it is too difficult to do alone. In this story it takes the cooperation of a really smart princess, a brave prince, and some good helpers to find the troll's heart.

The Troll with No Heart in His Body

ONCE UPON A TIME there was a king who had seven sons. The king loved his sons so much that when the time came for them to leave and look for brides, only the six eldest set off. The youngest prince remained at home for the king could not endure to be separated from all his sons at once. The other six promised to find a bride for their youngest brother as well.

They traveled far and wide until at last they came to a king who had six daughters, each more beautiful than the next. The brothers were so happy that they forgot all about their youngest brother and their promise. They were so much in love that they forgot their good sense and rode home using a shortcut over the mountains, past the castle of a mountain troll.

As soon as the troll heard the bridal party, he fell into a fit of fury.

"Who dares trespass on my land?" he roared and pointed his huge fingers at them. Immediately, the six princes with their six brides and the beautiful horses all turned to stone. It looked as though the troll had six stone statues in his courtyard.

The old king went nearly mad with grief waiting for his sons. Hugging the youngest, he said, "If it weren't for you I would have no reason to live."

"Oh, Father," said the youngest prince. "I too wish to go out into the world to seek my fortune. Who knows but that I may discover what has happened to my brothers as well."

The king was reluctant, but at last he gave in. He fitted the prince out as best

he could, but he had only a skinny old nag of a horse and a sack of food to give his son. With these provisions the prince rode off, waving to his old father.

After several days of riding he caught sight of a raven. This raven was so weak its wings dragged along the ground, and its feathers were dull and falling out.

"Please give me some food to eat," rasped the raven. "I haven't had a morsel for weeks. If you help me now, I will help you in your utmost need."

The prince looked at the raven. "I'm not so sure about the sort of help you can give me. But you are a sorry sight and I don't mind sharing my food with you."

As the raven ate, his wings grew sleek and strong. When he finished, he beat his wings, circled twice around the boy's head, and then flew off.

Next day the prince rode past a large salmon that flapped helplessly in the middle of the road. "Help me," gasped the salmon. "Please throw me into the river and I'll help you someday when you need it."

The prince shook his head a little and smiled. "I'd like to see what a salmon could do to help me! But you're surely not doing any good here in the middle of the road." He gently slipped the salmon into the river. The salmon swam up to the surface, gave a toss with his tail, and disappeared under the waves.

The prince rode on. The following day a wolf stood in the road. This wolf was so starved his ribs pierced through his skin and you could hear the wind whistling through his stomach. His fur hung in bits around him and he could scarcely keep his head above the ground.

"Give me your horse to eat," begged the wolf. "I haven't had a meal for two years. If you help me now, I will help you in your utmost need."

"No!" said the prince. "That's too much. I gave my food to a starving raven, I helped a salmon back into the river, but if I give you my horse to eat, how am I to travel?"

"Ride me! I will do whatever you ask, take you wherever you need to go. Just please, let me have your horse." Well, the wolf begged so long and so hard that the prince felt sorry for him and finally agreed.

While the wolf ate, his stomach filled in and his fur grew sleek and shiny. When he finished he lifted his head and looked at the boy with glittering green eyes. "Take the bit and the saddle and put them on me. You'll not be sorry for your kindness." Then the prince did as he was told, mounted the wolf, and away they flew as though the wind itself were taking them.

"Now tell me your errand," said the wolf. The prince told him about his brothers and his grieving father, and the wolf said, "Hang on, for I know just where to go." And they flew faster than the wind and in no time arrived at the troll castle.

"There stand your brothers and their brides," said the wolf nodding at the statues. When the prince recognized his brothers, terror gripped his heart.

"I might as well go home," said the prince. "How can I fight an enemy that can turn me into stone?"

"Don't give up! The troll who lives here is out hunting for the day, so you are safe now. Go inside. There you will meet a princess whom the troll has stolen. She will tell you what to do."

When the princess saw the prince entering the castle, she called out, "What are you doing here? It is sure to be your death. The troll who lives here is due to

come back soon."

"I've come here to kill the troll and free my brothers who are standing out there turned to stone, and I will free you as well."

"Don't you know?" asked the princess. "*Nobody* can kill this troll, for he does not carry his heart in his body."

"Since I've come all this way, I might as well try my strength," insisted the prince.

When the princess saw she could not make him leave she said, "Well, since you will not leave, we must try to do the best we can. Creep under the bed over there and listen well to what he says when I speak with him, and be sure to lie there as quietly as you can."

The prince crept under the bed, and soon the mountain troll came thundering home. As he filled the huge doorway, his nose shot up and sniffed the air. "I smell the smell of human blood," he roared.

"Yes, yes," said the princess. "A magpie flew by this morning and dropped a human bone down the chimney. I threw it out and swept the castle, but the smell lingers." That calmed the troll, and he sat down for supper. As they sat there the princess sighed and said, "There's one thing I want so very much to know, if only I dared ask."

"Well, what can that be?" asked the troll.

"I should so like to know where your heart is, since you don't carry it about you."

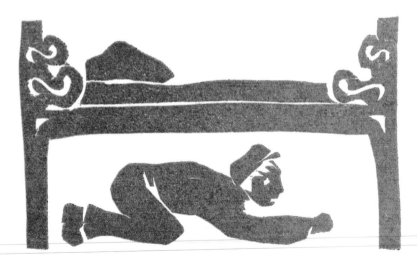

"Oh, that is one thing you needn't know anything about," said the troll, "but since you've asked, I keep it under the stone slab in front of the door."

"Aha, we shall soon see if we can't find that," thought the prince.

Next morning, as soon as the troll had left for the woods, the prince and the princess began to look for the heart under the stone slab, but they could not find it. "He has made a fool of me this time," said the princess, "but I will try again." She went out into the fields and collected all the prettiest flowers she could find and strewed them over the stone slab, which they had put back in its right place.

When the time came for the troll to return, the prince hid under the bed. Again the troll sniffed the air and complained about the human scent, but again the princess told him it was just the smell of a human bone dropped by a magpie. Then he noticed the flowers and wanted to know who had strewed them all over.

"Why, that was me, of course," said the princess.

"And why would you do a thing like that?" asked the troll.

"Well, you know how fond I am of you," said the princess. "When I knew you kept your heart there I just had to do it."

"OH HO HO," laughed the troll. "How could you believe I would keep my heart in a silly place like that?"

"How could I not believe, when you told me so yourself?" said the princess. "Where do you keep it then?"

"If you must know, it's over in the cupboard on the wall there," said the troll.

"Ah ha!" thought both the prince and the princess. "We will soon find it."

But the next morning, exactly the same thing happened. No matter how many cupboards they searched, they could not find the heart. "We must try once more," said the princess, and this time she hung garlands of flowers all over the cupboards. When the evening came the prince hid, and again the troll complained about the human smell. After the princess had calmed him, he noticed the garlands.

"What's the meaning of all this foolery?" bellowed the troll.

"Well, you know how fond I am of you. When you told me your heart is there I couldn't help doing it."

"How can you be so foolish and believe it?" asked the troll.

"How can I not believe it when you told me so yourself?" responded the princess. "I should very much like to know where it really is."

The troll could refuse her no longer and said, "Far, far away is a lake. On this lake stands a church, in this church there is a well, inside that well swims a duck, and inside that duck is an egg. Inside that egg, you'll find my heart. But it will do you no good to know this, for you will never go there."

"We'll see about that," said the prince to himself under the bed.

Early next morning the troll set out for the woods again. "Well, I suppose I might as well set off too," said the prince. Then he blushed and looked at the princess. "If I succeed and get rid of the troll would you be my bride?" he asked. The princess nodded and blushed too.

Outside, the wolf was waiting. "Jump on my back. I will find the way," he said when he heard what the troll had said.

Away they went, over mountains and fields and valleys until at last they came to the lake. The prince could not swim, but the wolf asked him not to be afraid. Then he plunged into the water with the prince on his back and swam to the island.

They walked ashore, and there in the middle of the island stood a church, just as the troll had said. But the church door was locked and the key hung high, high up on the steeple. The prince could see no way to climb up, but he wolf reminded him, "Now you must call the raven." And so he did! Immediately, the raven came, circled the steeple two times, took the key in his beak, and handed it to the prince.

In the center of the church was a large well, and in that well swam a duck. The prince called the duck until at last he lured her to him. Just as he caught the duck and lifted her out of the water, the duck let go of the egg and it dropped into the well.

Again, the prince did not know what to do, but the wolf reminded him, "You must call the salmon." He did, and the salmon came swimming through an underground river, and fetched the egg from the bottom of the well.

"Go outside and squeeze the egg," said the wolf. As soon as the prince squeezed the egg he could hear the troll roaring and screaming. "Squeeze it once more," said the wolf. This time the troll screamed even more piteously and begged

for his life. He would do all the prince wished, he said, if only he wouldn't squeeze his heart to bits.

"Tell him you will spare him only if he brings to life your six brothers, their brides, and their horses that he turned to stone," said the wolf.

The prince shouted the instructions. When the troll had restored the brothers, their brides, and their horses, the wolf said, "Now squeeze the egg to pieces." The prince took the egg between his two hands, lifted it high above his head, and squeezed it flat. Then they heard a tremendous explosion as the troll burst into thousands of pieces of rock.

The prince rode back on his friend the wolf, and when they got to the troll's castle, his six brothers and their brides stood there alive. The prince went inside the castle, fetched his own bride, and together they all rode home to the old king and the royal palace.

The king was so pleased and happy to see all his sons and their brides that he set about the wedding preparations at once. On the wedding day they had a grand feast. The king declared that never had he seen such lovely young people, but the loveliest of them all were the youngest prince and his bride. They should sit at the head of the table, the king said, for without their cleverness, none of them would be there.

Snipp, snapp, snute
Her er eventyret ute!

Snip, snap, snout,
This tale's told out!

From Asbjørnsen and Moe, "Risen Som Ikke Hadde Noe Hjerte på seg." This story so captivated me as a child that I can still remember the first time my father read it to me. I find it has the same power with American children. A heartless and nasty troll, high adventure, magic, a really smart princess, a persevering prince, and a seemingly insurmountable problem—this story has it all. My telling is close to the Norwegian. A story as good as this one does not need many changes.

Bibliography

Asbjørnsen, Peter Christian, and Jørgen Moe. *Norwegian Folktales.* Translated by Pat Shaw Iversen and Carl Norman. Oslo: Dreyers Forlag, 1960.

Asbjørnsen, Peter Christian, and Jørgen Moe. *Samlede Eventyr.* Oslo: Gyldendal Norsk Forlag, 1978.

Bettleheim, Bruno. *The Uses of Enchantment.* New York: Vintage Books, 1977.

Bø, Olav. *Trollmakter og Godvette. Overnaturlige Vesen i Norsk Folketru.* Oslo: Det Norske Samlaget, 1987.

Booss, Claire, editor. *Scandinavian Folk and Fairytales.* New York: Avenel Books, 1984.

Branston, Brian. *Gods of the North.* New York and London: Thames and Hudson, 1980.

Christiansen, Reidar Th. *Folktales of Norway.* Chicago: University of Chicago Press, 1964.

Dasent, George W. *Popular Tales from the Norse,* Edinburgh: Edmanston and Douglas, 1859.

D'Aulaire, Ingri, and Edgar Parin. *D'Aulaire's Trolls.* New York: Dell Publishing, 1972.

Haviland, Virginia. *Favorite Fairy Tales Told in Norway*. New York: Little, Brown, 1996.

Holbek, Bengt, and Iørn Piø. *Fabeldyr og Sagnfolk*. Copenhagen: Politikens Forlag, 1979.

Ingulstad, Frid, and Svein Solem. *Troll. Det Norske trollets Forskrekkelige Liv og Historie*. Oslo: Gyldendal Norsk Forlag, 1993.

Jones, Gwyn. *Scandinavian Legends and Folktales*. Oxford: Oxford University Press, 1956.

Klintberg, Bengt af. *Svenska Folksägner*. Stockholm: Bokforlaget Pan, 1977.

Kvideland, Reimund, and Henning K. Sehmsdorf. *Scandinavian Folk Belief and Legend*. Minneapolis: University of Minnesota Press, 1988.

Roll-Hansen, Joan, editor and translator. *A Time for Trolls*. Oslo: Nor-Media, 1962.

Simpson, Jacqueline, editor and translator. *Scandinavian Folktales*. London: Penguin, 1988.

Valebrokk, Eva. *Trollpakk og Andre Vetter*. Oslo: Boksenteret, 1995.

Sources

The folktales in this book are mainly from Peter Christian Asbjørnsen and Jørgen Moe's collection of Norwegian folktales titled *Samlede Eventyr*. From their first publication in 1841, these folktales gained enormous popularity, in part because their appearance coincided with a growing sense of national identity. Norway had achieved independence from Denmark in 1814 after four hundred years as a Danish colony. During this colonial period the official language of Norway had been closely modeled on Danish. Books were printed in Danish, and all higher education was conducted in Danish, causing, in a sense, the language and culture of Norway to go underground.

After independence Norwegians struggled to develop their own distinct identity, and the publication of the folktales became an important fuel for this national revival. The tales, which Asbjørnsen and Moe collected by traveling around the country, were felt to mirror the unique Norwegian landscape, with its towering mountains, craggy fjords, and deep forests. The eerie light, from endless daylight during midsummer to complete darkness during winter, is reflected in the clear contrast between good and evil, human and troll. The homespun sense of humor and the outspoken directness of the characters, from the peasant king down to the lowly Ashlad, revealed a stoic, no-nonsense approach to life felt to be typically Norwegian. In addition, the tales were recorded in the speech of the common folk, not in Danish. As such, these stories were the first works of literature published in Norwegian rather than in Danish.

Asbjørnsen and Moe's folktale collection became almost immediately a national classic. So important are these stories that whenever an official change

occurs in the Norwegian language, the first three books to be updated are the Bible, *The Official Book of Hymns,* and *Asbjørnsen and Moe's Collected Folktales.*

These are stories I have known since childhood. They were so important in my family that when I went off on my first day of elementary school, my father handed me a beautiful antique edition of the folktales as moral support. I received another lovely edition, this time in English, when I married my American "prince." It carries the following admonition: "To Lise with all good wishes and the hope that even though she may forget her Norwegian, she will never forget her Norwegian trolls." Well, I obviously never did. Within a year of beginning my life in America, I was telling troll stories, and I have never stopped since.

Like most Norwegians, I treasure the troll stories. Many of the tales in this collection have been part of my repertoire for more than twenty years. Most of them are close to the original Norwegian, but some changes have crept into the telling over the years. Since American children are not raised on trolls the way Norwegian children are, I have included more troll information. I do this both in the story itself as well as in my introduction to each story, just as I do in storytelling sessions.

In telling these tales orally I rely a great deal on my voice to show the character of the troll. To capture some of that in the writing, I have had to tell the stories out loud to myself as I type. This way I can tell when I whisper, when I roar, when I slow down, and when I speed up. All this I have tried to capture by choosing my verbs carefully, by using fewer and shorter words when I speak fast, or more words when I slow down. Throughout I have tried to keep the retellings simple and spare to clearly reveal the "good bones" of each story. This allows the powerful images

to stand out, and leaves plenty of room for the child's imagination to leap in.

Although there is some violence in these stories, I have resisted sanitizing them. Violence is an integral part of the stories. To remove it, is to remove the very threat the trolls pose and therefore the very real power that these stories have. Furthermore, my experience in storytelling has shown me that children are far less disturbed by the violence than adults are, and that, as psychologist Bruno Bettleheim has pointed out, children need this kind of imaginary outlet for feelings they may have themselves.

The Norwegian folktales were first translated into English by Sir George W. Dasent. His translations are an excellent English language source of the folktales. The reader can assume that all the stories from Asbjørnsen and Moe are found in Dasent's *Popular Tales From the Norse,* Edinburgh, 1859.

JUST TO HELP YOU REMEMBER WHAT SLOW thinkers trolls are, here's one last little story.

Trolls Shouting

One day a troll who lived in a mountain shouted: "There's a cow bellowing!"

Seven years later . . .

the troll who lived across the valley
answered: "Couldn't it just as well be a bull
as a cow?"

Another seven years passed . . .

before the troll in a third mountain, nearby, screamed, "If you two don't keep quiet and stop this commotion, I'll have to move!"

A Note from the Illustrator

MY GRANDFATHER, GUSTAV OLSEN, CAME TO CHICAGO FROM NORWAY in 1907, just before my father was born. When I was a girl I liked the meals my dad cooked of thin pancakes with lingonberries, a recipe from faraway Norway. In recent years I started to wonder what the stories of my own ethnic heritage were, other than Mickey Mouse, *Alice in Wonderland, The Secret Garden,* and *The Wind in the Willows.*

As I have lived on the land in northern Minnesota for thirty years, I have come to identify with the stories of the native people here and the way they tell the heartbeat and character of the land. Now I have discovered the troll stories, in which the rocks and rumblings have explanations in a similar way.

I visited Norway in 1993, and my thoughts of picturing the trolls in a book began. The west coast of Norway feels a lot like the north shore of Lake Superior, where I live now. This area was settled by Norwegian fishermen. The ones I know have the same sense of humor as the trolls in "The Handshake"; they help you out, but not without a joke or two to tease you.

The art for this book was done by making woodblock prints, carving the design into a flat block of wood, rolling colored ink onto the surface, and then printing onto paper. My son Jeremy Bowen applied his competent hand collaborating on the printing. I have used the great heritage of Norwegian woodcarving and design, particularly from the very old stave churches, in bordering the pictures. I have loved getting to know and respect the art of Theodor Kittelsen, the Norwegian illustrator who actually drew the trolls from life in the early 1900s.